Contents

KU-661-942

Acknowledgements

It has taken an extraordinarily long time for this book to come to fruition. It is almost twenty years since I first set eyes on one or two remarkably evocative images of the 1/5 York and Lancaster Regiment during research for my book on the Barnsley 'Pals' Battalions of the First World War and there were hints then that an extensive collection of rare images taken by a junior officer named Harry Colver during the Great War existed. Sir Nicholas Hewitt, owner of the *Barnsley Chronicle* newspaper, whose grandfather, Sir Joseph Hewitt, a South Yorkshire land and colliery owner, had served as the first commanding officer of the first Barnsley Pals Battalion, rescued a family album from a bonfire. In it were images of the 1/5th Battalion, Territorials , compiled by Sir Joseph's son, George who had been one of Harry Colver's friends and brother officers. But George Hewitt had not been the photographer. Another album turned up, featuring copies of the same images, then another – the Hess album – was deposited in the York and Lancaster Regimental Museum in Rotherham and revealed a few more before the Colver album emerged and it became clear that Harry Colver had been the driving force behind the images. A book was decided upon but other work intervened and the 'Colver' project was set aside. It was not until the 'Images of War' series was conceived by Pen and Sword Books that I felt a suitable vehicle had at last been found to bring the Colver images to life, nevertheless I owe a great debt of gratitude to several people without whom the book would never have been completed.

In the early days Roni Wilkinson – initially at the Barnsley Chronicle, latterly of Pen and Sword Books – expended an enormous amount of time and painstaking effort tracking down and then cataloguing many of the images as well as interviewing several veterans of the 1/5 York and Lancasters and their families. In designing this book – a task which he performs with the utmost skill and sensitivity for the subject matter – Roni claimed it was just like meeting 'old friends' and so it was. It has been such a pleasure to work closely with Roni again after such a long time.

I should also like to thank Peter Taylor, whose knowledge of the 1/5 Battalion was of tremendous help in the early days, as was the regimental knowledge of Stewart Eastwood and Don Scott, two past curators of the York and Lancaster Regimental Museum in Rotherham. I should like to record my grateful thanks to them for their unfailing courtesy and willingness to assist, all those years ago. The present curator, Karl Noble, has also been a source of help and encouragement as was Jane Davis, whose own project, cataloguing photographs for the regimental museum, also resulted in a book. I thank Karl particularly for his enthusiasm and willingness to set aside time for me to visit the museum's archives during a busy period for him and the museum, to whose Trustees I also extend my sincere thanks.

Sir Nicholas Hewitt and his son Charles, Chief Executive of Pen and Sword Books, have once again been very supportive of the project and I should also like to express my thanks to the families of the late Mr Robert Colver of Sheffield and that of his younger namesake, Mr Robert Colver, also of Sheffield, who responded to my several queries over the telephone with great patience.

Once again, my wife Heather and my daughter Georgia have been the epitome of support and understanding during the writing of the book. They truly deserve my thanks.

Every effort has been made to seek permissions where necessary but if, inadvertently, these have been overlooked I should be pleased to hear from copyright holders.

It only remains for me to say that if any errors or omissions reside in the book then they are entirely due to oversights on my part.

Jon Cooksey. Reading 2005

Introduction

IT COULD BE ARGUED that the images you are about to see on the following pages constitute a family photograph album. It is true that many of these rare and highly evocative images, the great majority of which have never before been published, deal with war rather than the more usual family snaps of birthdays, weddings and holidays by the sea, but it is a family album nevertheless. The family, in this case, was an infantry battalion of the part-time Territorial Force – the 5th, later renumbered the 1/5 Battalion, of the York and Lancaster Regiment. More specifically perhaps, the family consisted of the officers of that Territorial battalion, for in reading aloud the names of the officers, one could hear reflected the names of many of the most influential middle and upper middle class families of South Yorkshire. Here were the sons of the professional, business and landowning classes; the sons of 'Sirs' and solicitors, of Aldermen and JPs, families who lived not in houses but halls; families with wealth, with power and with influence. Many of these young men had been through the English public school system, a system which had inculcated an ethos of Muscular Christianity and the development of the virtues of duty, honour, sacrifice and service to King and Country. These young men were expected to become leaders and for those who did not join the Regular Army, service in the Territorial Force for home defence was the next best thing. There was perhaps never any question that they would not sign the Imperial Service Obligation, if war were ever declared, as indeed it was on 4th August 1914.

In any family album you will see a range of 'family' snaps – the paternal father figure of the 'old man' in command, gathering his young charges about him – group snaps of 'senior' family members, group snaps of 'junior' family members, pairs of best friends, images with seriousness and humour; of landscapes, horseplay, trophies and tragedies. It is all recorded in this military family album and it was recorded in the main by one man, a young junior officer called Henry Colver from Ranmoor in Sheffield, better known to the men in his army family as Harry.

It becomes apparent as one moves through the series of photographs he recorded for posterity, that Harry Colver had a passion for what was after all, a relatively new medium for the masses. Photographs of war were not new – the first ever 'war' photograph depicted a scene from the American – Mexican War which began in 1846 – and the photographs of Roger Fenton of the Crimean War and those taken by Mathew Brady's team during the American Civil War, broadcast the gruesome realities of conflict to a wider audience.[1] But the technology Colver was using was relatively new. Fenton and Brady had both used 'wet plate' technology with large, cumbersome cameras needing long exposure times but by the end of the first decade of the twentieth century many people, including Harry Colver, were amongst those in the first rank of the amateur photographers. These people had been bitten by the photography bug and had invested in much smaller, portable cameras using celluloid film, some of which could be slipped easily into a pack or tunic pocket as a means of recording their lives and the lives of those around them 'in real time'. It was Harry Colver who took his camera with him wherever he and his battalion went and it was Harry Colver who could be relied upon to take his camera from his pocket or pack and record the events of the day, no matter how busy or otherwise the battalion may appear to have been. It was also Harry Colver who, at times would come out from behind the camera to ensure his deeds were also recorded. There is also evidence in the following pages that Colver was not simply interested in 'pointing and pressing'. Several images demonstrate that he was actively thinking of composition in his framing of some of the photographs and at times he was not averse to organising men into various tableaux – a skill at which some of the earlier, professional war photographers had been very adept.

Colver had been with the 5th Battalion before the outbreak of war in 1914. Images exist showing him as a 20 year-old Second Lieutenant posing with his brother officers – at their annual two-week camp at Bridlington in 1912. Ironically he and his battalion were recalled from the annual camp at Whitby before war was declared and the then 5th Battalion was mobilised immediately. It was not long after that process of mobilisation had begun that Colver started to take his photographs. Here was a man who obviously wanted to capture every significant event of what he viewed would be the single greatest adventure of his and his young comrades' lives and share them with friends, for the photographs you see here have been selected from several sources.

It is obvious that Colver had the films developed and then either took orders for prints or allowed at least four of his friends to borrow the negatives they required to have their own set of prints produced. To date, images have been located in four albums and, as one might expect, many of the photographs were duplicated but there are several which are unique to one or other of the albums and which, for reasons unknown, do not appear in others. This made collation a painstaking task and establishing a chronological sequence was another in itself. Some loose prints have captions and dates while others were stuck into albums with no thought of chronology whatever. Whatever the reasoning behind the compilation of the albums there is no doubting the quality of many of these images. Several of the original prints are so sharp that much fine detail of the battalion's active service abroad can be observed using adequate magnification. It should also be remembered that these images were never subject to the 'dead hand' of official censorship by a high command fearful that British trench 'snaps' falling into German

Harry Colver

hands would provide them with useful intelligence. Colver does not appear to have been unduly concerned with any thoughts of censorship and neither, it appears, did his superiors bearing in mind the frequency with which they appear in this series of photographs.

And so, in April 1915, after a period of some six months training at home and on coastal defence duties in Lincolnshire, Colver and the South Yorkshire Territorials of the 5th Battalion York and Lancaster Regiment went to war to reinforce and plug the gaps in the Regular Army which, it is generally accepted, had virtually ceased to exist. Four months of hard fighting had drained its manpower and the Indian Army and many units of the Territorial Force had already arrived in France. The vast majority of the part-timers of the 5th Battalion leapt at the chance to serve their country overseas in the 'great adventure' and were soon on their way to the trenches of Flanders and the harsher realities of war on the Western Front.

John Keegan has remarked that, 'there are almost no private photographs of any episode of the First World War from any front. An event of the greatest historical importance, involving perhaps twenty-five million young men, many of whom owned cameras in private life and took 'snaps' of holiday, family and everyday life as a matter of course, yielded no photographic record at all except that captured by the official photographers'. [2] This book then fills a much needed gap and provides a rare and outstanding portrait of the 'great adventure' of war in Flanders in 1915, as seen through the lens of a young man who felt it his duty to serve and who was killed in action in the days before the mind numbing casualty lists of the Somme and Passchendaele.

Part One

Mobilisation

Six hundred red-coated soldiers of the 5th Battalion of the York and Lancaster Regiment trooping the Colour on the Queen's Grounds in Barnsley, (now part of Barnsley FC's Oakwell training complex) Saturday 27th June 1914. The 1/5 Battalion of the York and Lancaster Regiment, a regiment which, by 1914, drew the majority of its recruits from the heavy industrial centres of South Yorkshire, could trace its origins back to 1860, when two volunteer companies had been raised at Doncaster. Other companies were raised later and were eventually amalgamated to form the 8th West Riding of Yorkshire Rifle Volunteer Corps. In July 1881 – when, as a result of the Cardwell Army Reforms, the 65th and 84th Regiments of Foot had been paired off three months earlier to form the 1st and 2nd Battalions of the York and Lancaster Regiment – this unit became the 2nd Volunteer Battalion of the York and Lancaster Regiment. The early years of the twentieth century witnessed further changes to the structure of the British Army, particularly the nature of a force for home defence and under the Haldane reforms of 1908 the old Volunteer movement came to an end to be replaced by the Territorial Force. At that time the 2nd Volunteer Battalion of the York and Lancaster Regiment numbered twelve companies – one at Pontefract, three at Rotherham, five at Doncaster, two at Barnsley, and one at Wath-upon-Dearne – with a numerical strength of 1,123. A further rationalisation involved the absorption of one company into what became known as the 5th Battalion of the King's Own Yorkshire Light Infantry (KOYLI) and the compression of the remaining companies, along with two new detachments that were based at Treeton near Rotherham and Birdwell to the south of Barnsley, into a total of eight. These companies now formed the newly designated 5th Battalion York and Lancaster Regiment, part of the 3rd West Riding Infantry Brigade of the West Riding Division of the Territorial Force. On this occasion the men from those eight companies had paraded through the streets of Barnsley with bayonets fixed before proceeding to the Queen's Grounds where they were drilled for an hour and a half under the paternal gaze of their commanding officer Lieutenant Colonel Charles Fox. The event was reported in the Saturday 4th July edition of the local newspaper, the *Barnsley Chronicle*, which, whilst it conceded that their movements were, 'by no means perfect', congratulated Colonel Fox on his 'skilful handling of the battalion' and the 'smart appearance of the officers and men'. But it also revealed elsewhere in its pages that Territorial recruitment was down, no doubt one of the reasons behind the martial spectacle. It was only when the reader turned to page 6 of the same edition that they could read an account of the assassination of Archduke Franz Ferdinand, heir to the throne of Austria-Hungary, and his wife in the Bosnian capital of Sarajevo the day after the South Yorkshire 'Terriers' of the 5th York and Lancs had been put through their paces.

Thursday 6th August 1914. In front of the Old Corn Exchange on Market Hill, Barnsley's dignitaries turn out to give the 'Terriers' of the 5th Battalion a civic send-off. Listening to the Mayor, Councillor William Goodworth England, exhorting the men to do their duty and wishing them 'God- speed' on their mission are, from left to right, Councillor Chappell, Councillor Cockerill, Town Clerk Mr W P Donald (in the wig), Mrs England, Mr Joseph Hewitt, Reverend Richard Huggard and, wearing the rosette, Alderman Rideal. The assassination of Archduke Franz Ferdinand fomented the diplomatic crisis enveloping Europe and triggered a chain of events that eventually led to Britain's declaration of war on Germany two days earlier. Late July, early August was the time of the annual Territorial Force, two-week camp. In camp the part-time, citizen soldiers would live, work and train together for a fortnight before returning to their 'day jobs' and weekly drill and weaponry sessions. The companies of the 5th Battalion had been enjoying life under canvas at Whitby since 26th July when they were recalled on 3rd August. It was fortunate that they had been together, for when the order for mobilisation – in order to play its part in home defence – was received at battalion headquarters in Rotherham at 6.00 pm on the evening of 4th August, triggering the mailing of 896 'notices to join', it made the process that much easier. With the camp at Whitby struck many men made their way home for the last time to say goodbye to family and friends before parading again on 6th August for the journey to Battalion HQ.

Lieutenant Colonel Fox and more than 200 men of the two Barnsley companies listen to the speeches before marching to Barnsley station for the 3.30 pm Midland train to Rotherham and the Territorial HQ of the York and Lancaster Regiment with the sound of three cheers for the King, the Regiment and Colonel Fox ringing in their ears. The other outlying companies of the battalion made their way to Rotherham the same day and went into makeshift billets in the Doncaster Road and St Ann's schools.

After some four months training at home, during which time the battalion moved between its war station at Doncaster, Sandbeck Park in Rotherham, Gainsborough in Lincolnshire and the rifle ranges at Totley south of Sheffield, it was inspected by the Divisional Commander, Major General T S Baldock, as to its 'fitness for service abroad'. Four days later it was ordered to take over Number 3 Section of the defences on the North Lincolnshire coast. Battalion HQ was at North Somercotes and the eight companies were dispersed in villages along the coast. Time was spent manning trenches in the dunes, erecting barricades on the beaches, marching and looking out for spies but no threat emerged.

Second Lieutenant Aizlewood (left) and Lieutenant Alfred Carr man their 'trench'.

Lieutenants Carr (left) and Harry Colver brave the winds blowing off the North Sea. The battalion's strength on its move to the coast was 29 officers, 882 other ranks and 41 horses and it is interesting to note the fluctuations in manpower as drafts of men came and went. On 10th August 1914, the day the battalion had moved to its war station at Doncaster with a strength of 28 officers, 876 other ranks and 47 horses, Lord Kitchener had sent a memorandum to General Edward Bethune, Director General of the Territorial Force, enquiring how many Territorial units might be prepared to serve overseas and how many wished to remain in the Home Defence Force. Given that the Territorial Force's role was home defence, the men were then invited to sign the Imperial Service Obligation in order that they could serve abroad. A unit was deemed liable for foreign service when 80 per cent of a battalion's strength volunteered.[1] Whilst there might have been every expectation that a Territorial soldier would sign up for Imperial Service – indeed General Bethune himself reflected later that ninety two per cent of the Territorial Force had done so within a few weeks of the outbreak of war – not everyone, for various reasons, did.[2] In early September 1914, the 5th Battalion numbers had risen to 29 officers, 996 other ranks and 53 horses and another 175 recruits joined but 87 NCOs and men not signing the Imperial Service Obligation had been formed into a special company lettered 'K'. Again, on 5th December, one officer and 261 privates joined from the reserve battalion in Rotherham, while four officers and 148 NCOs and men for Home Service and those under 19 years of age – the minimum age for enlistment in the Territorial Force at the time was 17 as opposed to 19 in the New Army – departed to join the reserve battalion. In this way the threshold figure for Imperial Service was achieved against a backdrop of fierce competition for recruits as a result of Kitchener's appeal for volunteers for his New Army. The 5th Battalion was now set for service abroad and the re-designation of the Imperial Service, first Reserve and second Reserve units of the Territorial Force as 1st, 2nd and 3rd Line respectively had begun. Army Order III of 3rd January 1915 reorganised the battalion on a four-company basis and at the same time, being the parent unit, it was renamed the 1/5 Battalion, York and Lancaster Regiment, the nucleus of the 2nd Line and 3rd Line units becoming, respectively, the 2/5 and 3/5 Battalions.

The 1/5 had been relieved of its coastal defence duties on 25th February 1915 and boarded trains for York, a destination at which other units of the West Riding Division were congregating. No one was under any doubt that the time in York was to be spent in re-fitting for active service, indeed by 31st March it was generally known that the battalion was being 'readied for embarkation at an early date.'[3] More than twenty battalions of the Territorial Force had been sent to France by the end of 1914 to plug the gaps left in regular units after the fierce fighting of the first five months of war and by the end of January 1915 it had already been decided to send six full Territorial Divisions across to France in the order; North Midland, 2nd London, South Midland, West Lancashire, West Riding and Northumbrian. By the time of the group photograph on page 14, the North Midland, 2nd London and South Midland Divisions had already made the channel crossing and since the West Lancashire Division had been denuded of its battalions and was not ready to go, the West Riding Division was next on the list.[4]

Lieutenant Archie Paul (top of steps left), Lieutenant Alfred Carr (seated, bottom left) and Second Lieutenant J M L Hess (seated, bottom right) pose with their families on the steps of the Railway Hotel, York.

1/5 officers, including Lieutenant Carr (second left), Major Charles Willis (fourth left), Lieutenant Charles Fox, nephew of Lieutenant Colonel Fox (peering through the gap between cameraman and camera) and Captain Mallinson (extreme right), all laden with kit, gather curiously around a 'movie' camera outside York baths on the morning of their departure for France, 13th April 1915. After parading in England for the last time and saying their final farewells to family and friends who had made the journey to York to see them off, the remaining 28 officers and 930 other ranks left York station for foreign service on board two trains bound for Folkestone.

Lieutenant Colonel Fox gathers his officers about him for a formal photograph before leaving York on 13th April 1915 and proceeding to Flanders on active service. Seven of the group would be killed in action – three before the end of 1915 – and several more wounded to varying degrees during the course of the next three and a half years. There are some absentees, most notably the Second in Command, Major J E Knight, who, leading an advance party of three officers, 78 other ranks, 71 horses and 22 vehicles comprising the machine gun section and the regimental transport, left York for Southampton on 12th April and crossed to Le Havre the same night.

1. Second Lieutenant J R Handford
2. Second Lieutenant C E Glenn
3. Lieutenant G A G Hewitt (Killed 27.11.17)
4. Lieutenant J M Fisher
5. Lieutenant A Paul
6. Second Lieutenant G G Roberts
7. Lieutenant J S Hall RAMC
8. Second Lieutenant J H H Goodall
9. Lieutenant A G H Carr
10. Lieutenant E S Cattle (Killed 7.7.16)
11. Second Lieutenant H H Morrell
12. Lieutenant E A Barker, Quartermaster
13. Captain J G E Rideal
14. Captain H Parry-Smith
15. Second Lieutenant V G Southern

16. Second Lieutenant M H Goodall
    (Killed 14.7.16)
17. Captain A N Mallinson
18. Second Lieutenant W H Raley (Killed 14.5.15)
19. Captain T C Allport (Killed 1.8.15)
20. Captain E D B Johnson
21. Lieutenant H Colver (Killed 19.12.15)
22. Major C F Willis (Killed 8.3.18)
23. Lieutenant Colonel C Fox, Commanding
    Officer (1.4.14 – 28.9.15)
24. Captain T W Parkinson, Adjutant
25. Captain S Rhodes
26. Lieutenant W B Douthwaite
27. Lieutenant C D Fox
28. Second Lieutenant J M L Hess

Lieutenant Paul's men shoulder arms prior to inspection. On 18th February 1915 the Adjutant, Captain Parkinson, had noted in the war diary that the battalion had been re-armed with the 'Charger Loading MLE rifle designed to take Mk VII .303 ammunition'. The Regular Army were by now using the Short Magazine Lee-Enfield (SMLE) rifle but the Territorials were still armed with the older Long Lee-Metfords or Long Lee-Enfields which used the controversial Mk VI round-nosed ammunition. The re-arming referred to by Captain Parkinson, was the issue of 'converted' Long Lee-Enfields with chambers modified so that a charger could be used to reload clips of ammunition holding high velocity, sharp-nosed Mk. VII .303 rounds. Sighting alterations often went hand in hand with the conversion to using the Mk. VII ammunition causing the 1/4th (Hallamshire) Battalion of the York and Lancaster Regiment to have severe problems with the accuracy and performance of its weapons.[5]

Above: Leaving York. The men of A Company, some of whom have removed their hats, appear relaxed in front of the hand cranked camera after inspection. Company commander Major Willis (front right) looks pleased as Lieutenant Paul stands behind him with hands on hips prior to leading his men to the station

Opposite below: Large crowds gather to see the 1/5 leave York. A caption on the reverse of one print of this photograph, reads, 'The Baths where we paraded to march to the station', whilst on the reverse of another, in Lieutenant George Hewitt's hand, is written, 'The CO walking on parade when the battalion left York.'

.

Top left: York station platform and various officers wait to entrain for Folkestone. Lieutenants Carr (left) and Colver (right)

Top right: Captain E D B Johnson, commanding officer of B Company; stands in the centre of this group, pipe firmly fixed.

Below: A carriage awaits. Arms linked for a last snap before boarding. From left to right, Lieutenant Carr, Captain J G E Rideal, Lieutenant Paul, Lieutenant Colver and Second Lieutenant Hess.

Part Two

War in French Flanders – Fleurbaix

Lieutenant George Hewitt pictured here well equipped for the channel crossing. The battalion arrived at Folkestone on the evening of 13th April and made the crossing to Boulogne the same night. Arriving late they marched into Ostrehove Rest Camp under the shadow of the 'wireless station' on Mont Lambert and stayed there until 4.00 pm on the afternoon of 14th April, when they boarded trains for Hazebrouck. Detraining at 1.00 am on 15th April the battalion marched to Merville, twelve kilometres north of Bethune and some fifteen kilometres west of the front line trenches as the shell flies. There it rested until 9.30 am when it marched the seven kilometres northeast to the village of Doulieu, along with the 1/4 York and Lancaster Regiment and the 1/5 KOYLI, which together made up the 1/3 West Riding Infantry Brigade. There the billeting officers tried to find shelter in farms and cottages in and around the village.

The men pile arms and relax on the grass in an orchard in Doulieu behind Major Willis (left) and Lieutenant Colver who make themselves as comfortable as possible while the billeting arrangements are finalised. The history of the 1/4 Hallamshire Battalion recalled Doulieu as a 'pleasant little village...and in the glorious weather of that early Spring, with the fruit trees bursting into blossom and the peasants doing their business as usual, there was little to remind us of war save the occasional dull sound of a shell bursting down Neuve Chapelle way, the Verey lights at night, and the never-ending distant mutter of the guns at Ypres.' [1]

Doulieu. Major Willis (front) and two of his junior officers, Lieutenants Carr and Paul, catch up on their sleep.

Lieutenant Colonel Fox (left) established his battalion HQ at Lausages Farm in Doulieu and it was here that he learned of the plans for the gradual induction of his battalion into the mores of trench warfare in French Flanders. The West Riding Division, under Major General Baldock, had become part of Lieutenant General Sir Henry Rawlinson's IV Corps of General Sir Douglas Haig's First Army and Rawlinson, it appeared, was very impressed with the quality of the West Riding regimental and brigade officers and the rank and file, although the Divisional Staff had not made such a favourable impression. In a letter from Corps HQ in Merville to Lord Kitchener on 21 April he wrote,

'My Dear Field Marshal,
'I have deferred writing to you for the last fortnight partly because time has been short and partly because I wanted to see how the West Yorkshire Terl Div (sic) shaped - what with honours and rewards lists, reports on N. Chapelle (sic) and schemes for the future, there has not been a moment to spare. However now that our plan for the next move is practically decided on one has time to turn around - The W. Yorks Div. (sic) are certainly a fine lot of men with a very fair lot of Brigde Cmg (sic) officers but the staff is a bit weak and we shall have to lend them some staff officers who know their jobs - at present I am gradually introducing officers and N.C. officers as well as a proportion of the men, into the arts of Trench warfare — they go down and spend 24 hours at a time in the trenches alongside the regular battn now holding them and in this way gradually pick up the tricks of the trade — Baldock who commands the Divn (sic) is rather long in the tooth but he has a good experience and if we can get him to understand the practical side of soldiering he will do all right- at present he is too much addicted to theory but this will I hope vanish when he finds himself face to face with the Germans.' [2]

Opposite below: Officers congregate at Battalion HQ at Lausages Farm, Doulieu and discuss the impending move to the front line in small parties. The officer standing facing the camera with a cigarette in his mouth is Captain Thomas Coote Allport, second in command of B Company. Allport, from Dodworth near Barnsley, had been a director of the Wharncliffe Woodmoor Colliery, near Carlton, Barnsley before the war.

A vet examines a horse at Lausages Farm Doulieu. Although the British Army was one of the most highly mechanised that had ever been to war the horse still played a vital role in the transportation of weapons, equipment and supplies of all kinds. (Courtesy York and Lancaster Regimental Museum)

Almost there but not quite. Major Willis (left) and Lieutenant Paul wait patiently beside their makeshift bivouac outside a cottage in Doulieu. With almost 3000 men of three battalions to house in the vicinity of Doulieu delays in finding accommodation were inevitable.
(Courtesy York and Lancaster Regimental Museum)

A billet at last. Officers of A Company toast the fact that they finally have a roof over their heads beneath the gaze of religious icons and photographs of their French hosts on the mantelpiece. April 1915. From left Major Willis, Lieutenants Paul, Colver and Carr.

Major Willis and Lieutenant Carr change their headgear for a lark. Note the use of the groundsheet as a tablecloth.

A group of NCOs are pictured below with a French soldier captioned simply as 'Gideon' on the reverse of the print. Second left is Colour Sergeant Major J W Beaumont perhaps the most experienced NCO in the entire battalion. Between 18th and 25th April all the officers, NCOs and men went up to No. 5 section of the front line trenches east of the village of Fleurbaix in small parties for a period of 24 hours instruction in trench warfare attached to units of 25 Infantry Brigade of the 8th Division. It was during this induction period that the battalion suffered its first casualty – a man of A Company on 22nd April – followed by its first fatality on 27th April from wounds suffered two days earlier. 1717 Private Sam Mellor of B Company, an ex-Cortonwood Colliery coalminer, who lived with his widowed mother in Wombwell near Barnsley, was wounded whilst acting as a sentry on Sunday morning 25th April. He was evacuated to the 25th Field Ambulance, where he died on 27th April. His body now lies in Sailly-sur-la-Lys Canadian Cemetery. By the time Private Mellor had succumbed to his wounds the entire battalion had moved further forward into positions around Fleurbaix as a reserve for 25 Brigade.

Entente Cordiale. When not on duty in Doulieu the men of the 1/5 were able to meet and compare notes with their French counterparts.
(Courtesy York and Lancaster Regimental Museum)

Above: Men of A Company rest in orchards and pastures just outside Fleurbaix, the church a prominent landmark. Orders to move to Fleurbaix and form part of Brigade Reserve in Section No 5 had been received on 25th April and the move was made at 5.00 pm the following day. Battalion HQ, A, (Major Willis) B (Captain Johnson) and C (Captain Hugh Parry-Smith) Companies found billets east of Fleurbaix while D Company, under Captain Stephen Rhodes, established its HQ at Elbow Farm at the junction of the Grande Rue and Rue de la Chapelle less than two kilometres west of Bois Grenier. Elbow Farm was an entrenched position which effectively marked the start of the trench system.

Right: Battalion HQ at Fleurbaix. The commanding officer poses with officers of A, B and C Companies whilst a man tidies up behind them. From left, Lieutenant Colonel Fox, Captain Johnson, Lieutenant Colver and, on horseback, Captain Hugh Parry-Smith.
(Courtesy York and Lancaster Regimental Museum)

On the verge of their first full stint of front line duty, junior officers take turns with the camera to capture themselves in serious mood outside billets in Fleurbaix:
Lieutenant Paul (above)
Lieutenant Colver (above right)
Lieutenant Hewitt (right)

The battalion rested in cottages, farmhouses and barns in Fleurbaix from 27th – 29th April as spring advanced, and an unidentified officer of the Royal Engineers visited the battalion.

With the improving weather, some officers were able to take advantage of the rudimentary bathing facilities they found in the gardens of their billets. Second Lieutenant Hess sits in a farmyard trough while, from left, Lieutenant Colver, Lieutenant Carr, Captain Johnson and Second Lieutenant Handford look on.

After first stripping down to his Long Johns, Lieutenant Colver finds it easier to strip off altogether in order to get really clean.

From left to right, Captain Allport, Captain Rhodes, Lieutenant Fox and Lieutenant Paul.

Lieutenant Fox moves behind the camera to allow Lieutenant Colver (right) into the group.

Ready for the trenches. Senior officers of the battalion check their kit and pose for a final picture before leading their men 'up the line'. From left to right, C Company Sergeant Major Lumb, who was a member of the pre-war detachment based at the village of Birdwell, south of Barnsley, Captain Mallinson, Captain Smith (C Company), Captain Johnson (B Company) and Captain Willis (A Company). Two unidentified officers' servants are also invited into the frame. Company Sergeant Major Lumb, along with several other C Company NCOs, had already written to the Editor of the *Barnsley Chronicle* on behalf of the other NCOs and men of C Company on 25th April in which he spoke of their induction period.

'All of us have now been under fire from the Germans in the first line of British trenches, having occupied them alongside two famous regiments, namely The [1st Battalion] Rifle Brigade and The [2nd Battalion]

Royal Irish Rifles. We found these two regiments...very cheerful and happy and proved very good comrades. Their experiences were very valuable to us and put much heart and confidence in our fellows. It is very exciting sport shooting at the Germans but not very interesting when their snipers, who are deadly shots, send bullets whistling past our heads in rapid succession...Had you seen the weary troops struggling back to their billets after their turn in the trenches in the early hours of the morning you would have marvelled at their stamina and courage. The only complaint made was, "I'd give owt for a Woodbine."[3]

On 29th April, the German artillery shelled Fleurbaix for three hours from 9am until noon and again after lunch from 1.30 pm for an hour. This hindered battalion preparations for the move to the front line but it set out at 8.00 pm to relieve the 1/4 York and Lancaster Regiment (Hallamshires). The relief was completed by 11.00 pm without casualties in spite of the fact that the machine gun detachment came under heavy fire as it moved forward.

The caption on the reverse of the print below read, 'Path to trenches at Fleurbaix. Nearly always marked – a bit dangerous to walk on at times.' The exact route is not provided but given the location of the battalion billets and its destination – referred to in the war diary as 'No. 5 Section' of the trenches, which was, in fact, south east of the village of la Boutillerie – it is possible that the route to the trenches might have taken the battalion down the Grande Rue out of Fleurbaix, south east as far as Elbow Farm, before picking up D Company and then heading straight on along the track known as Road No.11. The trench system may have been entered near the building known as Tin Barn, that is, if the battalion had not entered the trench system around Elbow Farm or taken another route.

Lieutenant Colver is eager to record the battalion's first tour of duty in minute detail and takes his camera into the trenches for the first time at Fleurbaix. Two men of the 1/5 crouch beside a drainage ditch behind the front line trenches. This was just one of the hundreds of drainage ditches, dykes, culverts and even moated farms fed by the River Layes (Laies on early trench maps) and which criss-crossed this flat, low-lying region of French Flanders. The area around Fleurbaix, la Boutillerie and Bois Grenier lies at the very southern extremity of the geological belt known as the 'wet Flanders plain', founded on the Argile de Flandres – Flanders clay – before the ground starts to rise gently up onto the Aubers ridge. Flanders clay is naturally impervious and all rainwater is thus held close to the surface. Drainage from these flat lands is therefore very slow and the soils become very 'heavy' indeed during wet periods. Barton, Doyle and Vandewalle have observed that, 'to farmer and soldier alike, water has been a bugbear in Flanders for millennia: how to shelter from it, how to supply it for man, beast and machine, and how to get rid of it'.[4] The Layes flowed behind and almost parallel to the front line and at certain points it was less than one kilometre distant. The word 'river' was and still is rather a misnomer, for the Layes in this region is little more than a stream. Although behind the front line fire trenches, note the sandbags, corrugated panels and timber and wire-mesh barricades to screen British movements from German observers

A working party takes a break from digging and wiring, probably between the front and support lines. The war diary for 30th April – the first full day in the trenches – records the fact that 'nothing of importance occurred but snipers very active.'[5] These men are standing upright and there are reasonable fields of view across the flat landscape behind them, despite the two lines of sandbagged breastworks beyond. It is reasonable to suggest, therefore, that the image is taken looking back towards the British rear areas.

Another drainage ditch, this time with the 'right' bank built up and protected by a substantial sandbag and earth parapet. There are sandbags to the left. Possibly taken between the front and support lines.

Lieutenant Colver moves up and down the trenches to visit his brother officers, friends and men holding the line held by the 1/5. Here he takes his camera into B Company sector and has Lieutenant Cattle pose in shirtsleeves in support and communication trenches as Cattle's men go about their business. Because of the high water table in this part of French Flanders note that only shallow trenches are dug into the earth and the height is then achieved by building sandbagged breastworks held in place by a combination of timber stakes, interwoven wooden hurdles and wire mesh stretched over timber frames as reveting. The Official History claimed that many of the words used in relation to trench warfare, '...had in 1915 a value quite different to what they acquired later in the war. A "trench" was a slight narrow excavation with steep sides and six to nine feet wide traverses, lacking duck-boards and drainage and revetment worth the name', while a dug-out was '...merely a hole in the ground with splinter proof covering.'[6] The history of the 1/4 Battalion of the York and Lancaster Regiment remarks that , 'the trenches were bad and not bullet proof or connected up...the line consisted of a not too strong breastwork, weakened by dug-outs which were built into the bottom of it. There was no parados to any of the trenches, there were no communication trenches, and the nearest support line was a mile or more in rear.'[7]

The front line trenches at Fleurbaix, April/May 1915. The sector allotted to units of 3 West Riding Brigade extended from a point opposite the German held village of le Bridoux on the Bois Grenier – le Bridoux road, west to la Boutillerie, which meant that, given the kinks and curves of the trenches, the battalion had to defend more than two kilometres of the front line. Although the weather was dry at the time these photographs were taken, there was always work to be done in building up parapets in order to make them bullet and splinter proof.

Attempting to reinforce the parapets by applying themselves to sound trench construction was obviously a source of pride for the men of 1/5. The caption on the reverse of this image read, 'a bit of good work'

Rifles, ammunition and equipment lie in readiness on the sandbagged fire step of a very dry and very orderly fire trench.

An unidentified sergeant and corporal pose with men of a section of B Company to the right of a position referred to as 'the salient' on the reverse of several photographs of this period. There were two 'salients' of importance in this stretch of the line. The first bulged towards the German line astride the Bois Grenier-Radinghem road while the other lay further west, on the road from Fleurbaix to Bas Maisnil. In the vicinity of these salients the opposing front lines were some 100 -150 metres apart whilst in other sections the distance across No Man's Land increased to some 400 metres. In this case the 'salient' to which the photograph refers is the one on the Fleurbaix - Bas Maisnil road. Seated in front of the soldier holding the rifle is Private Charlie Williams from West Melton near Rotherham. The soldier on the extreme left holds a trench periscope – the only safe way to view the German line across No Man's Land.

Men at work in the fire trenches in the stretch of the line held by Lieutenant Colver's own A Company.

Another tidy trench. The caption on the reverse draws attention to the 'draining grids' on the floor of the trench. There is more equipment scattered around this time, including a mug, a pickaxe, a brazier and opened boxes. The man seated is holding what looks like a small wooden mallet, and has his feet either side of a large cooking pot. Note the man peering out from the shadows of the dugout at the far end of the trench. Just two layers of sandbags, probably placed over a corrugated iron sheet, provide bullet and splinter proof head cover.

A section of A Company sporting an assortment of headgear, tunics, different coloured shirts, and even a civilian waistcoat.

'Men's dugouts at Fleurbaix' reads the caption on the reverse of this photograph. Two dugouts nestle opposite each other in the angle of a trench. Because of the high water table it was impossible to burrow under the parapets to construct deep dugouts. Protection for officers and men from both the worst of the elements and the bullets and shells of the Germans, had to be built above ground in the same way as the breastworks. Here timber frames and iron sheets are pressed into service to provide additional reinforcement whilst three layers of sandbags covered with earth provide overhead cover. Note also the heavy blanket 'curtains' – drawn aside – which offered some measure of protection for the entrances of the dugouts.

A Company runners. On the left is Private Richardson. Company runners were key personnel attached to the various headquarters of a company. It was their job to deliver orders and messages from and to company HQ. When telephone lines were severed during severe German bombardments runners risked their lives trying to get messages through.

External and internal views of dugouts in the trenches near Fleurbaix

Inside B Company HQ. Captain Johnson and some of his officers relax surrounded by utensils, bottles and diverse supplies Left to right, Second Lieutenant Roberts, Johnson, Second Lieutenant Handford and Captain Allport.

Lieutenant Colver pokes his camera into Major Willis's A Company HQ dugout and allows bright sunlight to penetrate the gloom as Willis and his officers smoke after eating breakfast. Note the candlesticks made out of shell cases nailed to the timber support and the typically French coffee pot on the table amid the enamel mugs, bowls and loaves of bread. From left to right, Lieutenant J S Hall Royal Army Medical Corps, (RAMC), Lieutenant Carr, Lieutenant Paul and Major Willis.

Opposite below: To your respirators! A group of officers testing the first gas masks issued to British troops on the Western Front, some obviously taking a light-hearted approach to what was, in the light of very recent events, a serious matter - late April 1915. Standing left to right, Lieutenant Hall, RAMC, unidentified, Lieutenant Carr, Major Willis, Lieutenant Colver, Captain Rideal. Seated, Lieutenant Paul. The 1/5 Battalion had arrived in the forward zone virtually on the eve of the first chlorine gas attack in history, launched by the Germans on 22nd April against the northern flank of the Ypres Salient with the objectives of securing the village of Langemarck, the Pilckem Ridge and the line of the Yser Canal north of Ypres. The attack, part experiment to gauge how the deployment of the new 'chemical weapon' would work in practice and part feint to mask the transfer of men to the Eastern Front in preparation for the German offensive at Gorlice - Tarnow, was launched at 5.00pm on the afternoon of 22nd April with the discharge of dirty, greenish-yellow clouds of chlorine gas from 5,730 cylinders after a heavy bombardment. It drifted across No Man's Land on an east-west breeze, turning bluish-white as it roiled and spread towards fire trenches held by the totally unprotected men of the French 45th and 87th (Territorial) Divisions. The French line broke and within an hour thousands of coughing, vomiting French troops — many drowning in the fluid produced in their own lungs due to the effects of the chlorine — had evacuated the forward positions and were scrambling to the rear to escape the deadly vapours. By nightfall Langemarck and Pilckem village had been lost and the Germans had breached the allied line to a depth of over three kilometres across a front of more than eight, exposing the left flank of the Canadian Division. The situation was saved through a combination of unwillingness on the part of the German infantry to follow such an untried weapon too closely and the courage of Canadian and British troops, who dipped rags and socks in water and urine, clapped them across their mouths and noses and cobbled together what would later be acknowledged as a legendary defence. The line was thus held and despite another chlorine attack against the Canadians two days later the element of surprise had evaporated and the improvised defence buckled no further. The Ypres Salient had been saved.[8] The first masks being demonstrated here — note that Major Willis's and Lieutenant Colver's respirators are of a different colour and slightly different design to the rest — were little more than pads of cotton waste wrapped in muslin soaked in a solution of water, hypo or soda to help neutralise the effects of the gas and then tied around the head covering the nose and mouth. These were replaced in turn by the H (hypo) helmet, a grey flannel hood with a cellulose acetate window soaked in a hypo solution and, in November 1915, the improved P (phenate) gas helmet — this time with two layers of flannelette and glass eyepieces rather than the easily broken window — impregnated with anti-gas chemicals including sodium phenate and glycerine. Neither provided effective protection against phosgene gas and it would be phosgene, again delivered as a weapon for the first time in history by the Germans eight months later that cameraman Lieutenant Colver and the rest of battalion would encounter with deadly consequences in December 1915. To the right of the group are two metal tubes; signal rockets to be fired in the event of a gas attack.

Lieutenant Paul (left) and Lieutenant Carr become involved in a little horseplay with a large mallet and trench periscope outside Major Willis's dugout for the benefit of Lieutenant Colver behind the camera. An unknown brother officer, out of shot to the left, tries to get in on the act. The trench stores sign has been taken from elsewhere and put up for effect.

Colour Sergeant Major M J W Beaumont takes a break from duty to pose for Lieutenant Colver outside a dugout with Lieutenant Carr down the trench to his left. Beaumont, who became one of the battalion's most popular figures, was one of its 'old originals' and became one of its greatest success stories. He had joined the old 2nd Volunteer Battalion of the York and Lancaster Regiment in January 1901 and enlisted in the 5th Battalion on April 1st 1908 on the formation of the Territorial Force, being promoted Sergeant the same month. He attended the coronation of King George V in 1911 and was awarded the Territorial Efficiency Medal in August 1912, around the time of the 5th Battalion's annual camp, that year held at Bridlington. Thereafter his further promotion was rapid. He became Colour Sergeant in April 1914 and then Colour Sergeant Major in March 1915, just before the battalion went overseas. This was seen as a prestigious appointment for a NCO – the Colour Sergeant had been responsible for either defending the regimental colours in battle or leading the party protecting the junior officer carrying them – and thus the rank rewarded those sergeants who were able and greatly respected within their units. The rank of Company Sergeant Major or Company Quarter Master Sergeant gradually supplanted that of Colour Sergeant Major as the First World War progressed and Beaumont became recognised as the senior NCO of A Company. Beaumont's career did not stagnate in the trenches, however. He was selected to lead a party of NCOs to meet King George V during the King's visit to France in October 1915 and such had been his performance during the first seven months of the battalion's war on the Western Front that a month later he was gazetted Second Lieutenant. He then went on to serve the 1/5 with distinction for virtually the rest of the war – he spent six months in hospital during 1917 – being promoted Lieutenant in July 1917 and eventually acting Captain in April 1918, until he was captured during the crossing of the Selle on October 13th 1918. He

was repatriated to England a month after the Armistice. Beaumont was awarded the Military Cross in September 1916 for 'conspicuous gallantry' when, after an initial raid on the German trenches had failed, he led two platoons on a second which succeeded in breaking into the German line and bringing back a prisoner. He was eventually promoted Captain in June 1924.

Lieutenant Colver moves down the trench after snapping Colour Sergeant Major Beaumont to record the efforts of Lieutenant Carr in dugout construction. Beyond Carr, Major Willis looks up momentarily from his morning shave to check how his junior officer's work is progressing.

Lieutenant Colver (left) and Lieutenant Carr are seen here outside Captain Rideal's dugout in another part of the line.

Captain Rideal attends to his own early morning ablutions out of view of the Germans behind his dugout.

This photograph appeared in both the Colver and Mallinson albums. On the reverse of the Mallinson print was written,' My best friend, Mark Goodall. Wounded and died in action whilst on a raiding party July 5th 1916. Sgt. Crummock given DCM for carrying him back to Y & L lines.' Aged 21, Second Lieutenant Marcus Goodall was the son of the Reverend Canon and Mrs Goodall who lived at the Vicarage in Rotherham. He had been a senior prefect at Marlborough College before joining the Territorials of the 5th Battalion and going to war alongside Mallinson – Goodall is standing on Mallinson's right on the photograph of the 5th Battalion officers taken before their departure for France and Flanders – and his own brother. By the time of the opening of the Somme offensive on 1st July 1916, the 1/5 had journeyed south to play its part and Mark Goodall had become a captain. Contrary to the information given in the caption on the back of the photograph, Goodall did not die on 5th July. His date of death, according to the records of the Commonwealth War Graves Commission (CWGC) is recorded as 14th July and his place of burial as Puchevillers British Cemetery. The cemetery, a little to the west of Puchevillers, a village some 19 kilometres north-east of Amiens, is well to the rear of the Somme battlefields and was begun to bury those who had died whilst being treated by staff of the

3rd and 44th Casualty Clearing Stations which had set up near Puchevillers the month prior to the start of the offensive. Seriously wounded during the raid, Mark Goodall was taken as far as Puchevillers for treatment but never recovered and was buried in the first plot begun by those clearing stations. Although Lance Sergeant Crummock's actions in rescuing Goodall had ultimately been in vain he was awarded the Distinguished Conduct Medal for conspicuous gallantry in carrying wounded under fire both by day and night and for rendering 'gallant service' with his machine gun.

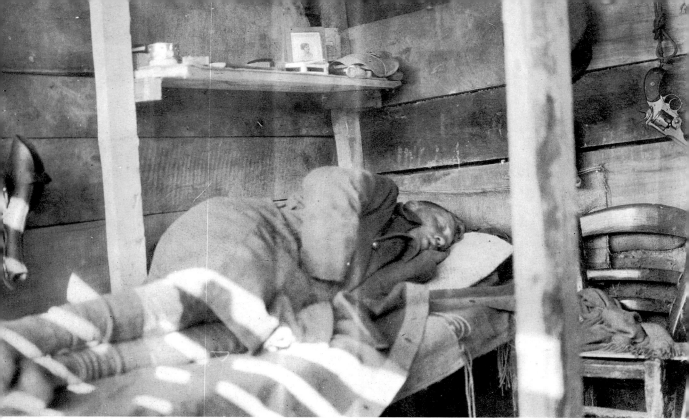

Sunlight streams into Lieutenant Alfred Carr's timber lined dugout as he snatches forty winks, fully clothed apart from hat and boots. Note Carr's Webley Mk.V .455 service revolver with its characteristic 'bird's head' butt, hanging by its lanyard top right

Lieutenant Paul (above centre right, standing with cigarette in mouth) and more than twenty men of A Company, display the remnants of uniforms and other items of clothing left hanging in the dugout and shredded by shell fragments during the explosion.

The first stint in the trenches ended at 10.30 pm on 2nd May when the 1/5 was relieved by the 1/4 York and Lancs and the battalion trudged back to billets in Fleurbaix. There the men rested in brigade reserve until the evening of 5th May when they in turn relieved the 1/4 in the same sector of the line. The war diary for the 6th May - the first day of the second full tour of duty - simply records that the battalion was in the trenches and that there were 'no important occurrences'. Photographs, illustrate what a narrow escape some men might have had that day as a large group (opposite below) sifts through the wreckage of a dugout on which, Lieutenant Hewitt recorded, 'an H E, 6'' shell made a direct hit – empty at the time.' Several photographs of this incident were taken proving how 'important' this particular 'occurrence', had actually been in the eyes of the officers and men who, obviously, viewed the damage caused as a novelty.

Part of the sandbagged, front line parapet destroyed by shellfire.

Major Willis (left) and Lieutenant Paul display a greatcoat, tunic and undershirt riddled by shrapnel as a result of the direct hit.

Second Lieutenant Hess (centre) makes the most of a quiet moment to ensure that his feet are dry as he, Second Lieutenant Roberts, (left) and Captain Johnson sit amongst an assortment of trench stores in rear of the position known as 'the Salient'. Although the weather during the time the battalion spent in the trenches of French Flanders was not unduly wet - the war diary refers only once to 'wet and cold' weather from 17th - 21st May when it was out of the line - it is obvious, from the examination of some of the photographs, that there were wet periods when the trenches became muddy. This is hardly surprising given the underlying geology of the area. The men of British units serving in this part of the line during the very damp winter of 1914-15 suffered terribly from the debilitating condition known as trench foot. Measures were implemented to issue gumboots or waders and to encourage men to change their socks and dry their feet regularly. During a tour of duty lasting several days, when washing and changing of clothes became more difficult, it was nevertheless essential to keep feet dry in order to prevent the onset of such conditions which could put a soldier out of action for long periods. If left untreated, severe cases of trench foot eventually led to gangrene and ultimately amputation.

Lieutenant Colver moves along the line to C Company sector and catches Captain Hugh Parry-Smith, in collarless shirt, cardigan and without equipment, waking up to another day of trench boredom.

Inset – Quite a contrast. Captain Hugh Parry-Smith, resplendent in uniform, prior to his departure for France.

A ubiquitous fellow. 'Doc' Hall (RAMC) pops up again, this time surrounded by officers of A and B companies.

Captain Parry-Smith holds a trench periscope and poses against the wall of a trench while some of his men crouch on the fire step to the right. The tall Captain is almost certainly leaning against the rear wall of the trench. Given the several references in the war diary to German snipers being 'active' during this time, he appears quite unconcerned that the top of his head is protruding above the sandbags of what must be the parados.

Turning a corner of a traverse, Captain Parry-Smith joins a small group of C Company men under Lieutenant C E Glenn, resting on the fire step. Parry-Smith looks out towards the German lines using his extendable trench periscope whilst another man operates a box periscope, fixed to the forward breastwork of the trench.

Lieutenant Colver frames Captain Parry-Smith in the doorway of his dugout as he sits down to write out a message on a notepad.

Right: Lieutenant C E Glenn.

Below: Captain Parry-Smith adjusts the sighting of a rifle on a specially designed rest which, using a system of mirrors like those used in a trench periscope and wires attached to the trigger, allowed the rifleman to observe and fire at the German lines and yet remain in the comparative safety of the trench without raising his head above the parapet. German snipers plagued the two York and Lancaster battalions in this stretch of the line and their activities are recorded in several sources. It was certainly not deemed safe to raise a head above the parapet during daylight hours. The history of the 1/4 Battalion records that the British 'loopholes' – specially reinforced positions from which a soldier might fire on the German trenches without being exposed – in this sector were, '...so obvious that it was no pleasant task to use them.'[9] Indeed, one of the Hallamshire's officers, Captain Ellison, is credited with inventing such a weapon with the aid of his Quarter Master Sergeant H L Cole.

'My Platoon – Some of the best' is scrawled on the back of this photograph. Nine men of Lieutenant Hewitt's platoon of C Company packed into a fire trench. The man in shirtsleeves in the foreground wears the wide belt and braces (shoulder straps) from his set of the 1908 pattern, closely woven, cotton webbing equipment with at least nine, full ammunition pouches, each pouch containing 75 rounds. Two clips of five rounds of Mk. VII ammunition lie on the fire step, bottom right.

Looking more like a group of mountain brigands than British soldiers, the same group of men are arranged into a suitably aggressive tableau a few moments later by Lieutenant Colver whilst Captain Parry-Smith continues to study the German lines with the aid of his trench periscope. The boxes just below the lip of the parapet are filled with bottles holding a solution of anti-gas chemicals used for soaking the respirator pads in the event of a gas attack.

The CO tours his battalion's trenches. Lieutenant Colonel Fox (left) in discussions with Captain Parry-Smith. C Company sector.

Having a chat with the 'lads'. The CO moves into the sector held by D Company under Captain Stephen Rhodes. Lieutenant Charles Fox (extreme right) sits on the fire step next to his namesake uncle. Hatless with spade to Colonel Fox's right is Lieutenant W B Douthwaite with a smiling Captain Rhodes next in line. It appears as though some of the other ranks have 'invented' a non-regulation form of lightweight headgear - 'chip bag' style - perhaps fashioned from sandbags.

Lieutenant Colonel Fox is joined by his Second in Command Major Knight as Fox moves into A Company sector. Major Knight (left) and Colonel Fox (leaning against the trench wall) point out some feature of interest, almost certainly to the rear as German marksmen would have punished any head appearing over the top of the trench. An A Company Runner looks at the camera while Lieutenant Colver takes the posed shot.

Lieutenant Colonel Fox removes his hat and enjoys a cigarette with an unidentified, visiting Lieutenant Colonel of the West Riding Divisional Royal Engineers.

Adjutant Captain Parkinson (left) and Second in Command, Major Knight looking extremely smart as they do their rounds of the trenches. Captain Parkinson – a regular officer – wears the ribbons of the Queen's and King's South Africa Medals, demonstrating his service in South Africa, during the Boer War, with the 1st Battalion of the Regiment some fifteen years earlier. He would be promoted to Major before the end of the year.

Scenes taken in the trenches of B Company.
Left: Captains Johnson (left, with trench periscope) and Allport.

Below left: Lieutenant Colver comes out from behind the camera for a change and sits on an ammunition box to have his photograph taken with, from left, Second Lieutenant Handford, Captain Johnson, Captain Allport and Second Lieutenant Roberts. Note the box of Mk.VII .303 inch, small arms ammunition 'in bandoliers', in the right foreground.

Below: Company Sergeant Major Dyson.

Captain Johnson with trench periscope and prismatic binoculars.

Hold it! Here comes the rum ration with an armed escort.

A working party under the command of Captains Allport (standing, first from the right) Johnson (standing, second right) and Second Lieutenant Handford (standing, fourth right) take time off for a 'brew up'. Lieutenant George Hewitt's caption for this photographs records that this was, 'the top of the salient in the Fleurbaix trenches – 170 yards from the Germans. Could be converted into Defended Post in case of attack.'

Opposite, below: 'Front of our trenches, April, May 1915. Taken from over the trenches and on the left barbed wire defences, put up or repaired each night. Germans 100 yards away in many places.' If this caption is accurate, and there is no reason to believe that it is not, given the relative positions of the barbed wire obstacles to the left, the earth excavated and piled up to form a rampart topped by sandbags to the right and the battered nature of the intervening ground, then this was risky shot to attempt. It would have been suicide to stand on the parapet and in any case the parapet appears too high in the image for Colver to have been standing upright when he took it. Perhaps Lieutenant Colver was so keen to get an image of what 'the salient' looked like from No Man's Land that he stood on the fire step, raised his arms above the parapet quickly, pointed the camera in the right direction then pressed the shutter and hoped for the best.

Lieutenant Paul and another, unidentified officer raise their rifles and try to bring down a German plane flying over the rear areas of the British lines. The caption reads, 'trying to pot planes - impossible!' Paul is using a Long Lee-Enfield while the other officer is using an early model Short Lee-Enfield. At least twelve spent cartridges lie on the bottom of the shallow trench. The 1/5 Battalion garrisoned the same stretch of front line trench, roughly half that allotted to the 1/3 West Riding Infantry Brigade, either relieving or being relieved in turn by its sister unit the 1/4 (Hallamshire) Battalion, York and Lancaster Regiment, until 26th June 1915. Relieved by the Hallamshires at 10.00pm on 8th May the 1/5 reported the situation as normal with the Germans 'apparently very inactive', firing just nine shells during the day. It then moved back with B Company in immediate support to the 1/4, HQ, C and D Companies at Elbow Farm and A Company in reserve in the trenches in front of Fleurbaix. At the same time the assaulting battalions of I, IV and Indian Corps were moving forward into their final positions prior to their assault on the German lines with the objective of driving through to seize the La Bassée – Lille road between La Bassée and Fournes-en-Weppes. What became known as the Battle of Aubers Ridge – the British effort being in support of a simultaneous French offensive fifteen miles to the south against the Vimy plateau – opened at 5.40 am on 9th May and units of the West Riding Division held the trenches to the north and south of the 8th Division which had concentrated its units for its initial attack against Fromelles. The Battle of Aubers Ridge – a battle that lasted little more than a day – cost the British in excess of 11, 000 casualties and sparked a munitions scandal back home. As the 1/5 Battalion was not in the line on 9th May it was never called upon to take part in the Battle for Aubers Ridge, indeed, it was never directly involved in any significant action during the best part of the two months spent in and out of the trenches near Fleurbaix, but it nevertheless continued to report a steadily lengthening casualty list of killed and wounded.

Captain Stephen Rhodes, the Commanding Officer of D Company. Captain Rhodes' connection with the battalion began in 1903 and he would eventually command it on active service before going on to carve out a distinguished post-war military career. At the time this photograph was taken he was two months away from a serious wound that would keep him out of action for more than three months. Returning to the battalion in October 1915 he would then take over the duties of Adjutant in November on the recall of the promoted Major Parkinson to Britain. After the Armistice he commanded the 1/5 until 1928 when he was promoted to command 147 (West Riding) Infantry Brigade. Captain Rhodes' brother was also an officer of the battalion.

Captain Rhodes assesses the performance of a Short Lee-Enfield Mk 1, (SMLE) rifle he has acquired as he takes aim at a target somewhere behind the front line. Several men, more used to seeing and handling Long Lee-Enfields, look on with more than a passing interest and wonder when they will be able to get their hands on an already coveted weapon. The SMLE appeared in experimental form in 1901 and the SMLE Mk.I officially saw the light of day in December 1902. After numerous modifications and conversions the Mk. III was approved in January 1907. The Regular Army went to war in August 1914 armed with the Short Lee-Enfield, which more than proved its worth in the BEF's first encounters with the German Army and it went on to become one of the most famous and recognisable military rifles of all time.

A Company officers' servants gathered round the kitchen table at Elbow Farm. Attending to an officer's needs and keeping him well fed was a key role and a good officer's servant had to be akin to a magician to conjure up the necessary stores and provisions to alleviate the monotony of a Western Front diet. The man on the right is an 'old sweat' – he wears the ribbons of the Queen's and King's South Africa Medals like Captain Parkinson – and had doubtless learned how to maximise the comfort of himself, his officers and comrades. On the table here are a number of opened cans including 'Natural No. 1 Peas', corned beef and jam. Two of the men are buttering bread and making sandwiches – (a large lump of cheese in one). Tinned pea and jam sandwich anyone? Note the coffee pot. It is the same one used by Major Willis in his dugout in the trenches. On the windowsill to the left are items of personal kit including hair and shaving brushes.

Out of the line. A Company officers enjoy a meal together in the comparative safety of Elbow Farm, although this image must have been taken at a time other than the period 9th -12th May. Elbow Farm was shelled sometime around midday on the 9th wounding three privates, 2128 W Thornton, 1984 Pte W Hirst and 2201 E Kendrick who are named in the war diary. Captain Parkinson attempts to record the names and details of all casualties during these early weeks of the battalion's experience on the Western Front but as the numbers increase he simply cannot keep up the practice. Between 17th and 22nd June, although the 'situation' in the trenches remained 'unchanged', the battalion lost three men killed – Privates Warren, Harrison and Greenwood and seventeen wounded, seven of those on the 19th June alone. The explanation was as follows:

'The above casualties, which are above the average usually incurred, were due mainly to snipers and to stray bullets from a distance. Most of them occurred behind the forward trench line in the neighbourhood of defended posts and reserve positions.'[10]

(Courtesy York and Lancaster Regimental Museum)

'Hugh's grave near Suicide Corner.' The preceding caption was written by Second Lieutenant Hess and records the burial location of Second Lieutenant Walter Hugh Raley – the first officer of the 1/5 to be killed on active service – who died of wounds on 14th May 1915. Hugh Raley was the youngest son of Lieutenant Colonel William Emsley Raley, a Barnsley Alderman and, at the time, commanding officer of the 14th (Second Barnsley) Battalion of the York and Lancaster Regiment. Lieutenant Colonel Raley also had another son, 30-year old Harry, serving in Flanders as a captain with the 2nd Battalion, Alexandra Princess of Wales's Own (Yorkshire) Regiment – the Green Howards. Second Lieutenant Raley was signals officer attached to Lieutenant Colonel Fox's HQ and after three days in brigade reserve went back into the line with the 1/5 on 12th May. At 3.00 pm on the afternoon of the 14th, Raley – 800 metres behind the front line and making his way forward by road to the trenches to lay out telephone wires – was hit in the right side by a sniper and died of his wound that evening. He was buried in Y Farm cemetery – a cemetery begun only two months prior to Raley's death – south east of Bois Grenier. It is interesting to note that on some of the earliest trench maps of the sector, there is no reference to a 'Suicide Corner', a name that may simply have had local currency and the farm at the same location as the present day Y Farm cemetery is marked as 'Wye' Farm. The death of their youngest son affected Lieutenant Colonel Raley and his wife Elizabeth greatly, indeed Mrs Raley died 'of a broken heart' soon afterwards. She was thus spared the pain of mourning her eldest son on 15th June, just one month after Hugh's death. The loss of his wife and two sons in the space of a month broke Lieutenant Colonel Raley's health and he stepped down from command of the 14th York and Lancs. Captain Harry Raley has no known grave. His name is commemorated on the Le Touret Memorial near Festubert, just 14 kilometres south west of his younger brother's grave at Y Farm.

Out of the line again the 1/5 found that the name of their division and brigade had changed. As of 15th May the West Riding Division became known as the 49th (West Riding) Division, and the 1/1, 1/2 and 1/3 West Riding Infantry Brigades were renumbered 146, 147 and 148. That said there was little else that changed for there was no time for any rest and relaxation worth the phrase. There were always the inevitable working or ration parties to be made up of men from battalions 'in rest' and these would make their way towards the forward trenches at night with all manner of stores and supplies, sometimes digging, repairing or wiring trenches in the support lines as well. During the day there was always some digging to be done even if that meant road repairs. Billeted in farms, barns and outhouses behind the British front line, some of whose owners were still living in the main house – the men of the 1/5 would take time to scrape mud from their uniforms and equipment, clean their weapons, take part in drill and – almost Heaven itself – wash themselves. The attention to detail obviously had the desired effect in maintaining discipline. On 12th June a message was received by Major General Baldock at Divisional HQ from the Adjutant General at GHQ, to the effect that:

'The Commander-in Chief [Sir John French] notices with gratification the record of the 49th (West Riding) Division for the month of May, which shows that no single conviction by Court-Martial has occurred, a condition which does not obtain in any other Division of the Armies. He desires that his appreciation of this fact be duly conveyed to the 49th Division.'

As General Officer Commanding First Army , Sir Douglas Haig also wished to, ...*'add an expression of his great satisfaction at the state of discipline in the 49th (WR) Division, and also desires to congratulate the Division on its soldier like bearing and efficiency.'* [11]

Left: Captain Stephen Rhodes poses outside a thatched, farm cottage near Fleurbaix.

Above: Madame supplies buckets of clean water and towels and looks on as two soldiers wash themselves down in the yard of the same cottage.

(Courtesy York and Lancaster Regimental Museum)

As the entry in the war diary for 9th May confirmed, Elbow Farm – just two kilometres behind the front line as the shell flies – and some of the other billets were well within range of the German artillery. Lieutenant Charles Fox is seen left posing out in the open next to an almost perfectly circular shell crater with the sub soil thrown up by the explosion forming a raised lip around the rim. Note the flat nature of the terrain in this part of French Flanders.

(Courtesy York and Lancaster Regimental Museum)

Right: Regimental Sergeant Major John Henry Rowan takes an early morning smoke outside his billet and is captured forever on film. He has just three months left to live. A highly experienced NCO, 46-year old Rowan, from St Philip's in Sheffield, was to die of wounds received on 12th August 1915 in an explosion near Battalion HQ on the Yser Canal north of Ypres. Between the 11th and 15th August German trench mortars would be 'very active' and would take a heavy toll, killing twelve, including Rowan, and wounding thirty-five others. Rowan is buried in Talana Farm cemetery, a cemetery begun by the French in April 1915. There are many more men of the West Riding buried alongside RSM Rowan in plots III and IV. By the time the battalion's two month tour of duty in this region of French Flanders came to an end on 26th June 1915, one officer, Hugh Raley, and eleven men had been killed with another officer, Lieutenant W B Douthwaite, and 48 men wounded; a total of 61 casualties.

(Courtesy York and Lancaster Regimental Museum)

This letter sent to the local weekly the *Barnsley Chronicle* is dated 25th April 1915 and appeared in the paper a month later. Sufficient information is supplied to assist German military intelligence in plotting troop movements and dispositions.

Packed up, saddled up and ready to go. Lieutenant Carr (left) and Lieutenant Colver take final snaps outside their billets in Fleurbaix.

BARNSLEY TERRIERS.

LOCAL MEN IN THE FIGHTING LINE.

TO THE EDITOR OF THE "BARNSLEY CHRONICLE."

C. Company,
1/5 York and Lanc. Regt.
West Riding Division,
British Expeditionary Force.
C/o. G.P.O. London.
April 25th, 1915.

Sir,—We were much gratified when we received last week's "Chronicle" to read your interesting article relating to our departure from York to "Somewhere in France." We arrived in France all safe and sound and after a most interesting journey under very peculiar and unusual circumstances we arrived at our destination very close to the firing line. All of us have now been under fire from the Germans in the first line of British trenches, having occupied them alongside two famous regiments, namely the Rifle Brigade and the Royal Irish Rifles. We found these two regiments who have been here since the beginning of the war very cheerful and happy and proved very good comrades. The value of their experiences was very valuable to us and put much heart and confidence into our fellows. It is very exciting sport shooting at the Germans but not very interesting when their snipers, who are deadly shots send bullets whistling past our heads in rapid succession. We are very pleased to tell you that we are fortunate enough to have had no casualties yet. Our baptism of fire came much earlier than anyone at home expected, although we ourselves knew to expect it. We are now prepared to face the enemy as often as we are required. Although we are not wishing to underate the enemy's ability we think and have confidence that we shall not fail to give them as good a fight and beating as our comrades of the regular army are doing day by day. We are very well supplied with food but our greatest regret is that we cannot get for either love or money that inexpensive but luxurious "Woodbine." This is our continual craving but we can get no satisfaction. Tobacco and cigarettes are issued to us twice weekly but is is all what is known as the "swank cigarette," and any kindly disposed person who would care to supply us with a few packets would be the recipient of our most heartfelt thanks.

Had you seen the weary troops struggling home to their billets after their turn in the trenches, in the early hours of morning you would have marvelled at their stamina and courage. The only complaint made was "I'd gie owt for a Woodbine."

Tender our best wishes and thanks to all our friends in Barnsley and district who have so kindly and thoughtfully remembered us whilst serving our King and country since the beginning of the war.—For the N.C.O.'s, men of C. Co., 1/5 York and Lanc. Regiment.

G. LUMB, C.S.M.
W. H. SMURTHWAITE, Co., Q.M.S.
G. WHITE, Sergt.
C. JACKSON, Sergt.
J. F. DOUGLAS, Sergt.
P. SMITH, Cpl.
E. RIDDIOUGH, Cpl.
A. E. BRETTONER, Pte.

Captain Stepehen Rhodes (right) and his brother Lieutenant Geoffrey Rhodes prepare to ride out to the next phase of their war. On 25th June, HQ received Brigade Operation Order No 7 which stated that 148 Brigade would be relieved by 25 Brigade of the 8th Division the following night and then move a little way south with the remainder of the Indian Corps to a line running south from the village of Picantin to north of Givenchy. At 9.45 am the next day the battalion turned its back on the trenches of the Fleurbaix and Bois Grenier sectors for the last time and marched the nine kilometres to Sailly-sur-la-Lys, where it bivouacked for the night. But the move south never happened. Instead the 1/5 was transferred to the VI Corps (Lieutenant General Sir J L Keir) of the Second Army, then commanded by a man who had seen action in the Sudan and South Africa as an officer of both the 65th Regiment (which became the 1st Battalion) and the 2nd Battalions of the York and Lancs and had risen to command an Army – General Sir Herbert Plumer. Instead the battalion headed north by stages and by 1st July were billeted or bivouacked on the road between Watou and Poperinghe where General Plumer – relatively new in post having recently been elevated to command Second Army on the sacking of General Smith-Dorrien after the Second Battle of Ypres – inspected the Division on 3rd July followed by Lieutenant General Keir two days later.

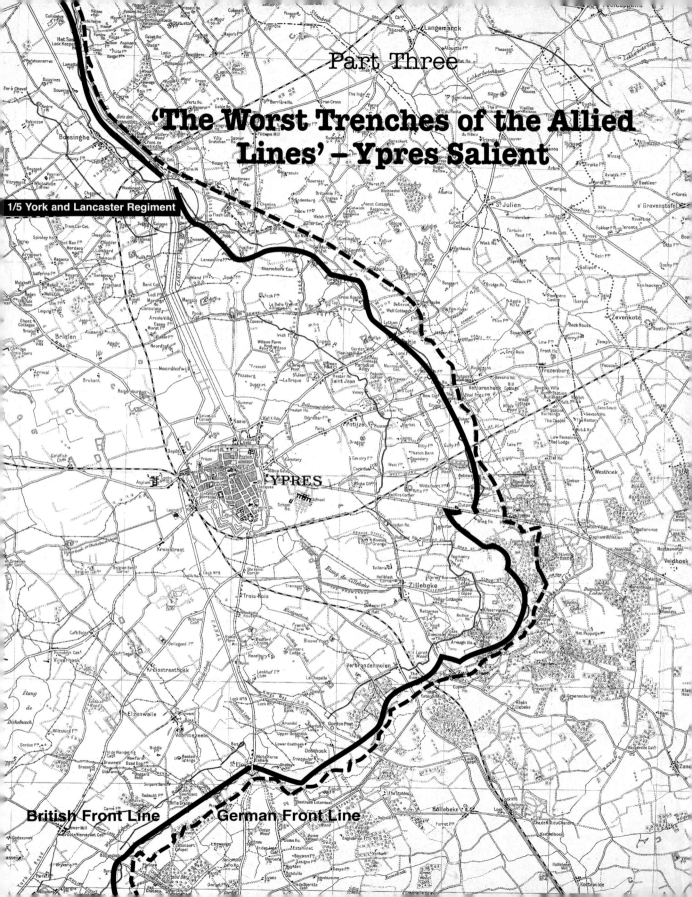

Part Three

'The Worst Trenches of the Allied Lines' – Ypres Salient

1/5 York and Lancaster Regiment

YPRES

British Front Line   **German Front Line**

Vigorous inter-company and inter-platoon sports when out of the line, were an excellent way of maintaining fitness and developing the aggressive, competitive spirit which the High Command desired to see imbued in the British Army. Captain Parry-Smith, on the right holding the white handkerchief, is seen here umpiring a very serious round of tug o' war. Most unusual for this series of photographs – the majority of which are of excellent quality – there is a faint double exposure and the ghostly images of three legs can be seen centre left.

On 8th July the battalion marched to a rest area in Oesthoek Wood near Poperinghe and set up bivouacs. Captain J M Fisher (right) and the promoted Lieutenant Hess are pictured riding amongst the tent lines and hutments in the wood.

The horse-drawn 1/5 York and Lancs officers' mess cart trundles into Oesthoek Wood.

Before their Mess is organised several officers take a snack *al fresco* using upturned boxes as seats and what appears to be a fence panel or hoarding as a makeshift table. From left to right, Lieutenant Paul, Captain Fisher, Lieutenant Hess, Lieutenant Colver and Captain Johnson.

'The path to the trenches near the Yser Canal.' The track was known as 'Fleet Street' and the straight course of the Yser Canal is marked by the second line of trees running across the shot in the distance. The line of trees nearest the camera marks the course of the River Yperlee – also straightened – a little less than one kilometre west of the canal. There was no time for the battalion to get used to the fresh air and open spaces of Oesthoek Wood Rest Camp for it had been ordered to prepare for garrison duty of the trenches to the north of the Ypres Salient. It set out on the evening of 9th July and marched via the village of Elverdinghe to the banks of the Yser Canal, where it 'took over the trenches on the left of the British line recently captured from the Germans by 11 Brigade near Boesinghe.'[1] So began a two month stretch in a sector which the Hallamshire's historian later dubbed, 'as nasty piece of front as the British occupied in the summer of 1915.'[2] The 4th Division, of which 11 Brigade was a part, had relieved French troops in the line now to be held by the 1/5 Battalion, just a month earlier. The trenches, originally dug by the Germans and subsequently captured by the French, were found to be in a shocking state with unburied corpses, both French and German, lying out in the open. The German line facing 11 Brigade included strong points known as Farm 14 and Fortin 17, both screened by International Trench. 600 metres beyond were strong secondary positions and further still lay the Pilckem Ridge, offering the Germans unrivalled observation of the allied line. It was decided that an attack be made on International Trench, Farm 14 and Fortin 17 to reduce pressure on the left of the British line by creating more depth between the front line and the Yser, whilst at the same time diverting German attention from the vicinity of Hooge. 1st Battalion The Rifle Brigade was selected to make the attack with 1st Somerset Light Infantry in support – with zero hour set for 6.00 am on 6th July. The attack commenced with a ferocious artillery bombardment at 5 am – incredibly an 18-pound field gun had been manhandled into the British front line and fired over open sights during the barrage. An hour later the Rifle Brigade went over and captured International Trench with few casualties at which point the Somersets moved up in support. Farm 14 remained in German hands and although they attempted to organise two counter attacks in order to recapture International Trench, 11 Brigade held on to its gains, thereby advancing the British line in the sector by some 70 metres, across a 300-metre front.[3]

Men in sandbagged support trenches near the Ypres-Boesinghe road, again near Fleet Street and to the east of a locality known as Hull's Farm. Hull's Farm was named after Brigadier General Hull, commanding officer of 10 Infantry Brigade, but who, due to the heavy losses and confusion in British units during the bitter fighting of the Second Battle of Ypres, found himself in command of a composite unit – named simply Hull's Force – made up of men from disparate regiments. The Yperlee is 150 metres to the east, beyond the, none too imposing barbed wire fence. The hand over was completed by 1.30 am on the morning of 10th July and the battalion shook out as follows: Battalion HQ was established on the west bank of the Yser Canal, near a bridge numbered and lettered '6D', and opposite the ruins of South Zwaanhof Farm, A Company moved to hold the right flank of the battalion front while B Company was entrusted with the centre which included holding a forward trench on the Pilckem road. C Company was in support of the centre on the canal bank. D Company took responsibility for the left flank along the east bank of the Yser Canal. And here was the rub; there were no troops to the left of D Company. The front line trenches on Captain Rhodes' extreme left ran, quite literally, into the dried up course of the Yser Canal, only beginning again on the opposite – west – bank where they were held by French troops. This junction – just south of the railway bridge across the Yser at Boesinghe and on a bend in the canal – was the very point at which the Ypres Salient began its long sweep southward. D Company of the 1/5 York and Lancaster Regiment now had the dubious distinction of propping up the extreme left flank of the entire length of the British line in France and Flanders and it proved to be a particularly unhealthy position. Nephew of the CO, Lieutenant Charles Fox later recalled that his company were '...stuck on the very end of the Salient, on the banks of the Yser...in a terrible position. And by far the worst spot was on the extreme left flank, for it meant that the enemy was on the front and the side of you. Which of our four [platoons] would get the worst spot? We decided to toss a coin for it – I lost!'[4]

Looking back towards Boesinghe. One can make out the stationary line of railway trucks in the distance. Given the angle of the line this photograph was probably taken in the vicinity of Hull's Farm.

Although the battalion war diary mentions that HQ was on the west bank opposite South Zwaanhoff Farm, it is believed, given the angle of shot and the available evidence, that this photograph shows the ruins of North Zwaanhof Farm on the east bank of the Yser Canal. North Zwaanhoff farm was only 200 metres north of its more southern namesake and although bridge 6D, also mentioned in the war diary, is between the two, it was closer to North Zwaanhoff Farm, being only 50 metres away. One of the buildings on the horizon in the centre is believed to be Glimpse Cottage on the road running north to its junction with the Boesinghe-Pilckem Road.

The Yser support line. A rough, tough looking bunch of A Company men led by Colour Sergeant Major Beaumont, hatless in the centre, engaged in the construction of a solid looking shelter using an existing brick built culvert.

On their way to the trenches on the west bank of the Yser Canal the men first had to cross the Yperlee River which flowed into a bend on the Yser Canal just south of the railway bridge at Boesinghe. Funk holes were dug into the east bank of the Yperlee for the sentries. A man's head and shoulders are just visible to left centre and note the compacted soil of the path along the riverbank from thousands of boot strikes.

Scenes on the Yser Canal taken towards the German lines from the west bank and from the east bank looking back towards the British support, reserve lines and headquarters areas. Note the trees felled by shellfire.

Lieutenant Colver moves up and down the bank and records several bridges spanning the Yser.

A bridge over the Yser Canal, believed to be of Bridge 6D, with shelters dug into the reverse slope of the east bank. The canal is almost dry in this particularly wide section of its course but deeper on the far side of the bridge.

Above: Another view of the same bridge shown on pages 90-91, this time taken from the vicinity of Battalion HQ on the west bank looking northeast towards the line of trees on the Boesinghe – Wieltje road and the German lines on the Pilckem Ridge beyond.

Left: Another bridge but this time with screens erected along its length to confound prying eyes. View from the east bank looking back towards the British rear. Lieutenant Charles Fox remembered that first trip into D Company sector on 9th July, which was completed in the early hours of the 10th.

'My first trip into the sector was by night, it had to be; the Germans could see every movement. The nearest bridge crossing the canal to get to my sector was 500 yards away – and that used to get blown up every day by shellfire. The engineers had to go in every morning to repair it [so that troops could go over at night].[5]
Lieutenant Fox thought the sappers, *'wonderfully brave. The finest fellows I've seen.'*

Two photographs of the left flank of D Company, the sector manned by Lieutenant Fox's platoon and the point where the Ypres Salient began in the north. Lieutenant Fox recalled that this view showed the back of D Company trenches.

The photograph opposite above, is taken a little further to the right of the one below and with the camera raised slightly. This is a print from the collection of Lieutenant Hess and it shows more clearly the muddy boundary between the armies of three nations created by the draining of the Yser in this sector. The French line started on the left bank amongst the trees with foliage and Lieutenant Hess has marked the start of the British front line with a white dot and that of the Germans with a white cross. It seems incredible but at that point the two sides were separated by not much more than fourteen metres. In addition to the wire entanglements strewn with tin cans placed on the canal bank behind the British trenches, the British drew trench covers, made from barbed wire stretched across timber frames, over their trenches for extra protection against German patrols or raids.

'My platoon was near the leafless tree on the right of the photograph.' Fox recalled. *'The German trenches started at the next tree with the leaves on. Barbed wire strewn with tin cans was piled into the almost empty canal behind us to alert us if the Germans tried to get around the back of us during the night. The French were facing the Germans on the opposite side of the canal.'*

These photographs record the furthest point on the extreme left of the entire British Army in Flanders during the summer of 1915.

Les Allies. Lieutenant Colver wanders over to the west bank and enters the trenches in the French sector just south of where the railway bridge crossed the canal. The French soldier in the foreground is very difficult to spot and easy to miss. He has his head down – kepi on – so his face is not visible, his right hand is behind his neck and he has his rifle with fixed bayonet on his right hand side nearest the camera. A British soldier can be seen further along the trench.

Lieutenant Colver lathers his face and prepares to shave while Major Willis rests on the bank to his right. Although A Company took over the right flank of the battalion front it is clear that this image is not taken whilst Colver was in the front line.

Dawn in the trenches. Lieutenant Colver takes a smoke break with an unidentified sergeant after an obviously chilly night in the line given the greatcoats and headgear. Note that the rifle is cocked ready for firing. This indicates the very dangerous section of trenches that the Territorials were occupying.

Trench breakfast. These A Company officers appear to be enjoying their breakfast of bread and jam and tea. From the left, Lieutenant Cattle, Major Willis, Lieutenant Alderson, (seated), Lieutenant Aizlewood and Lieutenant Carr. The group appear in jovial mood and this image is certainly not taken on their first morning in the trenches near the Yser canal, 10th July 1915, as the battalion's introduction to the war in the Ypres Salient was anything other than a jovial experience. Lieutenant Fox later recalled that this area was an absolutely filthy place with mud everywhere.

'I got into this trench and waited for daylight. As it grew lighter I stuck my periscope up over the top of the trench and a terrible sight met my eyes – there were piles of dead in front, in the narrow strip of No Man's Land…the smell of decaying flesh was awful, and there were the flies. The trenches we were occupying once belonged to the Germans and we had to pass through B Company to get to our sector and on the way you had to pass this certain dugout. Inside were three dead Germans in sitting positions…and they had become horribly bloated. Eventually we shoved earth in on top of them to cover them up.'[6]

The battalion war diary paints much the same picture, the only shreds of good fortune coming in the form of abandoned weapons and equipment. *'The trenches … were in a terrible state. Several of them had only recently been captured from the Germans and very little had been done to consolidate the position. A large number of dead were still unburied both of our own [and] of the enemy and the conditions in which the officers and men had to live were terrible. The trenches and canal bank were strewn with rifles and equipment belonging to killed and wounded of the units previously in occupation of the line and with ammunition, bombs and stores of every description. These were collected as far as possible and depots formed at different points. A number of men re-armed themselves with short MLE rifles and long bayonets in place of their CLLE rifles and short bayonets.'[7]*

The Germans were still smarting from their ejection from International Trench four days earlier and were intent on retaliation. Snipers concealed in cottages at the east end of Boesinghe bridge, from where they could enfilade the British line for 800 metres, were a constant threat but it was the shelling which did the most damage. During the whole of the day the 1/5 were subjected to a bombardment the severity of which they had never before experienced and with much heavier calibres of shell. The parapets were blown in, in several places and a machine gun position was struck, overturning the gun and burying most of the team, one of whom was killed and one wounded. The casualties for this period – 10th and 11th July – were very heavy indeed, amounting to 27 men killed, Captain Stephen Rhodes and 127 men wounded with two men unaccounted for. It is a much-overused phrase but in this case appropriate to record that the 1/5 endured a baptism of fire. .The number of dead recorded on the battalion's first two days in the Ypres Salient was more than double the total for just over months in the Fleurbaix sector, with the figure for wounded pushing towards three times the Fleurbaix figure. Consequently newspapers in South Yorkshire bore the heavy tidings that their Rolls of Honour for that week were 'of larger dimensions' than at any period during the war. Three men, Corporals J Yates and A Calvert and Private A Gwynette, were later awarded the Distinguished Conduct Medal for their actions during the bombardment of 10th July either in attending to wounded men under fire or in rallying comrades when many other NCOs and men had been killed.

PRIVATE CARL WHITE.

SERGEANT A. E. BLACKSHAW.

THE INCREASING ROLL OF HONOUR

LATEST ADDITIONS TO THE LOCAL LIST.

BARNSLEY TERRITORIALS' TERRIBLE TOLL

OVER ONE HUNDRED CASUALTIES.

Since our last issue, the rumour which had for several days previously been prevalent in Barnsley that the local Territorials had suffered acutely in action, has received undoubted verification as the details which we give below show.

Many of our brave lads have forfeited their lives in the defence of their King and country, though even as we write the precise number of victims has not been officially announced.

Our Roll of Honour on page 8 is this week of larger dimensions than at any period during the War, and that list is very incomplete.

All the lads who have fallen were well known locally, and the utmost sympathy—a sympathy in which we join—has been extended to their bereaved families. We give the photographs of a few of the heroes; other photographs have reached us too late for insertion in this issue, but these will appear next week.

We can assure our readers officially that the Territorial casualties were between 120 and 150. The two trenches which they were ordered to occupy were filled with German dead, and the sight—to use the words of one Barnsley lad—" was simply horrible." The Territorials were shelled all the way to the trenches, and many were wounded before they reached the goal. "A" Company, for instance, had 6 killed, 35 wounded, and 2 missing. Some of the officers were hit, but none were killed, and, happily, none were wounded.

After the incidents on the 10th July, General Dawson highly complimented the Territorials, and said "they had stuck it splendidly."

PRIVATE ROYCE LINTON.

PRIVATE J. DOCKER.

PRIVATE TOM BAILEY.

SERGEANT G. E. LEDGER.

SERGEANT JOE SWAINE.

CORPORAL F. RIDDIOUGH

PRIVATE W. WOOD.

PRIVATE WALTER BRADLEY.

PRIVATE JOHN WHALLEY.

PRIVATE J. FARMER.

The 11th July proved to be 'a much quieter day' but the battalion had taken such a battering the previous day that it was decided to take it out of the line after some 48 hours. It was relieved by 1/4 York and Lancs and marched back to the grounds of Elverdinghe Chateau, where it went under canvas 'for a much needed rest'. Keen amateur photographer that he was, Lieutenant Colver took the opportunity to record several images around Elverdinghe and here he composes peaceful scenes of Elverdinghe Chateau and lake and dappled, woodland glades alongside less uplifting images of Elverdinghe Church gradually being destroyed by German heavy artillery. It is worth noting that the chateau and its grounds were also within range of the German guns.

Elverdinghe Church was easily ranged on by the German artillery spotters and was gradually being destroyed by heavy artillery. (Courtesy York and Lancaster Regimental Museum)

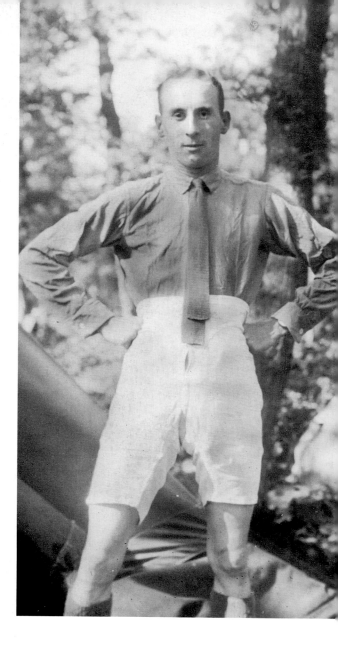

12th July 1915, the first morning out of the trenches. Lieutenant Colver comes out of his tent and asks his batman to capture the transformation wrought by a shave, wash and brush up.

After putting on the rest of his uniform Lieutenant Colver tours the camp for more subjects. Here he takes a portrait of the Padre, Sidney Barnes.
(Courtesy York and Lancaster Regimental Museum)

Lieutenant Paul poses with German booty. He wears a line infantry pickelhaube – although it is difficult from the quality of the print to make out if it belonged to an officer, senior NCO or man – and displays a greatcoat, left behind by the Germans after 11 Brigade attack on 6th July and recovered from the trenches. Prisoners of the 215th Reserve Infantry Regiment of the 46th Reserve Infantry Division are known to have been captured during the attack.[8]

The Colonel's quarters. Lieutenant Colonel Fox stands outside the doorway of his tent beneath the trees in the grounds of Elverdinghe Chateau.
(Courtesy York and Lancaster Regimental Museum)

Above: Major Knight snapped during a walk in the countryside surrounding Elverdinghe.

Right: Major Willis takes his turn to pose outside the Colonel's tent.

Below: Lieutenant Colonel C C Moxon, (second on the right), the commanding officer of the 1/5 KOYLI, also of 148 Infantry Brigade, pays a visit to his colleagues of the 1/5 York and Lancs whilst they are in bivouacs at Elverdinghe. Joining him during a stroll through the woods are, from the left, Captain Parkinson, Lieutenant Colonel Fox, and, extreme right, Major Willis.

McMahon Farm. After another tour in the line from 14th – 17th July and another spell in brigade reserve at Elverdinghe Chataeau from 18th-21st July, A and B Companies were sent forward to support positions at McMahon and Malakoff Farms while HQ, C and D Companies remained at the chateau. For the next three days, the men went out on night working parties digging communication and support trenches and carrying rations forward to the front line. McMahon and Malakoff Farms were just 400 metres apart on the road from Elverdinghe to Boesinghe and some three kilometres from the Yser Canal and so it was no difficulty for the officers of A and B Companies to visit each other.

'McMahon Farm, July 1915', is George Hewitt's caption to these photographs. Hewitt, on the right in both photographs, now wears the insignia of a captain and he is seen here in jocular mood with, from left, Captain Johnson, Lieutenant Handford and an unidentified padre.

Another man takes the camera and Lieutenant Colver, left, joins the group in a much more serious study.

Another photograph of McMahon farm but indoors this time, as staff from Battalion HQ arrive for discussions with the commanding officers of A and B Companies. Major Knight clutches a sheaf of documents and there are more documents on the table. What, at first sight appear to be bottles of wine, are, on closer inspection, bottles of Perrier table water with the distinctive Perrier lettering. It was actually an Englishman, St John Harmsworth who, in 1903, first leased from Dr Louis Perrier and then bought, the natural spring in France from which the mineral water flowed. Harmsworth named the spring after Perrier, who had put so much effort into developing it. Looking for a return on his investment, Harmsworth needed a unique and easily recognizable product. He already had a name: 'Perrier', but he needed a design for the bottle so he turned to the Indian clubs he used for exercise for inspiration. Harmsworth knew that if he could convince the British Amy in India of the qualities of his water he could conquer the remaining British colonies. His sales pitch worked and following its success in the colonies, Perrier water was served at Buckingham Palace and Harmsworth was granted the coveted 'by appointment' status. Standing, left to right, Lieutenant J H H Goodall and Captain Fisher. Seated round the table, left to right, Captain Johnson, (B Company), Lieutenant Colonel Fox, Major Willis, (A Company) Major Knight, a promoted Lieutenant Hess and Adjutant Captain Parkinson.

The group moves outside and gathers outside the doorway leaving Captain Fisher just inside. From left to right, Captain Parkinson, Lieutenant Hall, Major Knight, Lieutenant Colonel Fox, Major Willis, Captain Johnson, Lieutenant Hess and Lieutenant Goodall.

Modder Farm, a few hundred metres west of Hull's Farm, was one of several to bear names associated with the war in South Africa at the turn of the nineteenth century. One of the farm buildings has two shell holes in a gable end. On the night of 25th/26th July the battalion moved up into brigade support with Fox establishing his HQ at Saragossa Farm. B and A Companies moved into the dugouts to east and west along the Yser Canal bank, while C Company manned the trenches near Hull's Farm and D Company occupied Modder Farm. From these positions work continued on strengthening the second line trenches. Four days later the battalion relieved 1/5 KOYLI – and began work on connecting up parts of the front line.

THE STRICKEN BRAVE.

CAPTAIN ALLPORT KILLED IN ACTION.

OTHER LOCAL HEROES FORFEIT THEIR LIVES.

Many painful sensations have been experienced in the Barnsley district since the war broke out. Week after week comes the sad tidings of some of our local soldiers having forfeited their lives in the greatest of all

CAPTAIN ALLPORT.

causes, and this week is no exception as our portrait gallery too plainly shows. The news of Captain Thomas Coote Allport of the 1/5th Y. and L. Regiment (Barnsley Territorials) having been killed in action on Sunday night was received in Barnsley and Dodworth with deep sorrow. Captain Allport, was the third son of Mr. Howard Aston Allport, J.P., and the late Mrs. Allport, of Dodworth Grove, and letters concerning his death intimate that he was in the trenches when an attack was repulsed. A wounded German was left in front of the British trench, and his appeal for help caused much concern to Capt. Allport, who was looking over the parapet to see the whereabouts of the man when he was shot through the head. The captain only returned to the front the previous Tuesday, after enjoying a short leave.

BARNSLEY TERRITORIAL CASUALTIES.

Appended is a list of the casualties sustained by the 1/5th Y. and L. Regiment (Territorials):—

KILLED.

Anderson, 2399 H. H.
Bailey, 2316 T.; Barnish, 1842 W.; Bartholomew, 2261 E.; Bassett, 2493 T.; Bradley, 1442 W.
Cloke, 2258 W.
Docker, 2578 J.
Foster, 2680 W. J.
Goldthorpe, 1064 J.
Haley, 1473 J.
Jacques, 292 T.; Jones, 1841 Cpl. F. W.
Kilner, 1325 H.; Knowles, 1829 J. W.
Ledger, 347 Sgt. G. E.; Lewis, 2064 C.; Linton, 2051 R.; Lloyd, 2097 Cpl. E. J.; Long, 2200 G. W.
Nixon, 1515 H.
Purser, 1993 J.
Smith, 2613 L.
Whalley, 395 J.; White, 2490 T. C.; Wilson, 3142 B. H.

WOUNDED.

Allen, 2467 Lce.-Cpl C. H.; Avison, 2158 M.
Badham, 1106 A. E.; Bagnall, 2239 E.; Bagshaw, 471 S.; Barker, 1731 Drummer E.; Barson, 2714 W.; Binney, 109 Sgt. S.; Blackshaw, 351 Sgt. A. E.; Bourne, 261 Lce-Sgt L.; Briggs, 2545 J. H.; Brocklesby, 2398 S. W.; Burns, 1858 Lce.-Cpl. J.
Carradice, 2246 S. B.; Castle, 2353 H.; Catley, 46 Sgt. A.; Charlesworth, 2503 V.; Chesworth, 1808 C.; Child, 2641 J.; Collins, 2667 G. E.; Cook, 1457 Drummer W.; Cooke, 2222 H.; Copley, 1451 W.; Cutts, 2567 C.; Dolan 2339 T.; Doylan, 2111 J.
Ellis, 356 E.; England, 2407 H.; Exley, 2207 J.
Feers, 723 G.; Fenton, 2255 F. W.; Fretwell, 2003 W. J.; Froggatt, 2291 J. W.;
Gallagher, 2386 J.; Gash, 1859 J.; Gilbert, 1521 Cpl. G. H.; Gilbert, 2471 H.; Greasley, 2136 A.; Green, 2379 J.; Griffiths, 1935 W.; Gunn, 1615 J. L.
Haigh, 1334 H. E. D.; Haigh, 2166 J. W.; Haywood, 2071 F.; Heppenstall, 2370 C.; Hirst, 2228 H.; Hirst, 2118 T.; Howarth, 2236 J. A.; Hudson, 290 Lce.-Cpl. T.; Hunter, 1642 F.
Jackson, 2229 J.; Jackson, 2354 T. H.; Johnson, 1902 C.; Jordan, 221 E.; Large, 2013 Drummer T.
Lawton, 2444 J.; Laycock, 3093 Lce-Cpl. J.; Liles, 2507 H.; Loates, 2308 A. G.; Lomas, 1621 Lce-Cpl. J. B.; Lyman, 2324 W.
McKay, 1898 Drummer C. J.; McNaught, 2007 W.; Machin, 1031 Sgt. W.; Manship, 2345 Lce.-Cpl. S.; Martin, 1066 Drummer J. A.; Medlock, 217 Sgt. J.; Miles, 1092 G.; Mitchell, 2392 H.; Mite, 76 R.; Moore, 1444 Lce.-Cpl. F.; Morby, 2592 J.; Murray, 79 Cpl. H.
Nixon, 2290 J.;
Oliver, 1689 B.; Osborne, 2120 G.
Paskell, 2362 E.; Peace, 1698 G.; Perry, 2150 T.
Quinn, 2637 L.
Roberts, 3222 Lce-Cpl. H.; Roundhill,

This series of three photographs (beginning previous page) show Captain George Hewitt's dugout on the Yser Canal sector. Hewitt's own caption reads, 'my dugout, Yser Canal, last week in July 1915.'

Right: Lieutenant Cattle squeezes in between Hewitt and Colver.

Below: The trio retreat into Hewitt's dugout to demonstrate the living conditions inside.

These photographs were taken just two days before Captain Hewitt was seriously wounded. In the afternoon of 1st August he received a head wound from a sniper's bullet. In a letter home to his mother, written on 6th August, he described the incident:

'I was sniped in the trenches and it was very annoying for it was the last time and place I would have expected to get hit. I was just on my way to have some food in my dugout, when suddenly I saw millions of stars and found myself on my knees clawing air! I never lost consciousness, and after they had put about four field dressings on (I bled like a pig) I walked down to the Aid Post after all sorts of anxious moments – the Boches followed me out with a couple of whizz-bangs.'

Coincidentally, Hewitt's father, Lieutenant Colonel Joseph Hewitt, was, at the time on a two-week commanding officer's course in France aimed at familiarising New Army COs with the realities of trench warfare. Visiting his old friend Charles Fox on the Yser sector he heard the bad news of his son's wound and, abandoning the tour, dashed around tens of hospitals in France trying to locate him. He found him at last, head swathed in bandages, in the Westminster hospital in Le Touquet and the case notes on the clipboard at the foot of the bed told its own story of how close George had come to death. 'Large gutter wound in occipital region splitting scalp right down to the bone, exposing skull.' *The official description of the wound is bad enough'* George wrote, *but I do not think it is as terrible as it sounds, and I am simply not worrying about anything know – except coming home when I am fit enough."[9]*

Captain Hewitt, head still bound in bandages, convalesces in the garden of the family home, Ouslethwaite Hall near Barnsley, with sister Kitty and dog Scamp. Hewitt would return to France to join the 2/5 Battalion of the York and Lancaster Regiment in the 62nd (West Riding) Division but would not cheat death a second time. He would be killed in action on 27th November 1917 during the Battle of Cambrai. Hewitt has no known grave; his name is inscribed on the Cambrai Memorial to the Missing at Louverval. 1st August 1915 proved to be a cruel day for the officers of 1/5. Not only did they suffer the loss of George Hewitt with a serious wound but also the death of the popular Captain Thomas Allport in an apparent attempt to help a wounded German. On the night of 31st July the men holding the trenches held by C Company were alerted to a small party of Germans attempting to cross No Man's Land, probably with the intention of bombing the garrison. One of the bombs exploded prematurely before the Germans reached the British wire, obviously wounding one of their party, for in the minutes that followed the explosion lone cries for help were heard coming from somewhere out in No Man's Land. Early the next morning Captain Allport decided that he would try to get the man back into the British trenches. Lifting his head above the parapet to locate the wounded man's exact position, a sniper's bullet struck Captain Allport's head, killing him instantly. Captain Allport, aged 33 and unmarried, was the third son of Mr Howard Aston Allport J P and the late Mrs Allport of Dodworth Grove to the west of Barnsley and had been with the 1/5 since 1908 at the time of the reforms. He had only returned to the front line four days prior to his death after a short period of leave.

Two photographs of Lieutenant Harry Colver taken in International Trench. The move into a trench so recently captured from the Germans was obviously an event of some note for Lieutenant Colver and his brother officers. After all, the line had been advanced and the Germans had been driven out of their positions. Colver was obviously keen to come out from behind the camera and have others record images of himself in the fairly confined spaces of the old German line.

Below: 'Harry in old Boche dugout.' Although the height is restricted, note the very solid construction of this shelter with sturdy timber supports and timber lining throughout. German dugout construction was the result of a psychology based on holding on to existing gains and therefore building for permanence whereas the allies were – initially at least – loathe to invest time and resources into constructions which might be deemed to be 'permanent' lest this should detract from their intention of advancing to regain occupied ground. Is that the ubiquitous A Company coffee pot in the entrance to the dugout (right front)? This particular photograph is not especially sharp due to the low light levels in the dugout but there are what appear to be two photographs on the wall behind Colver. Did these belong to the previous occupants?

Left: Behind the camera once again. Lieutenant Colver asks Lieutenant Hess to pose for a snap in International Trench. Note the large shell case suspended from the wooden frame to Hess's left pressed into use as a 'gas gong' to alert the men in the event of a gas attack.

A unique series of photographs looking out over the parapets of the International Trench across No Man's Land towards the German front line. Between 30th July and 2nd August there was much work scheduled for the improvement and consolidation of the front line, especially connecting up certain sections which had been damaged by both British and German shellfire. After a period of wet weather, which inevitably led to muddy conditions and hampered progress, the weather had improved enormously, drying out the ground thus allowing a considerable amount of work to be done.

Below: The new British forward trench is just beyond the camera marked by a line of sandbags running across the photograph from left to right. Beyond that one can see an old German communication trench, now running across No Man's Land. The new German front line can be seen in the distance as another line of sandbagged breastworks, behind a few 'chevaux de frises' barbed wire obstacles, running left to right just in front of the two tall trees in the mid distance. View looking east.

International Trench is marked by the line of raised earth running away from the camera to the right in this image. The sandbagged breastworks marking the new British forward trench snakes off towards the top left. Note the debris – including several tin cans, a long iron bar which looks like a rail, old sandbags and items of clothing – to the right of the barbed wire obstacle in the foreground. Previous occupants have simply thrown some of this over the parapet but it appears as though the area has been disturbed, perhaps by a shell strike during the heavy German bombardment of 10th July. View southeast.

Two views taken from different spots in the same, narrow communication trench, running towards slightly higher ground to the left of the 1/5 front and clearly showing the hard work still to be done to make it passable. Note the left thigh and right, booted foot in the foreground of image opposite, which is all that we can see of the man laying on the floor of the trench. View looking northeast.

The 1/5 spent the best part of the next five months moving in and out of the line, taking their turn at front line duty on the sector allocated to 148th Brigade; sometimes in support, sometimes in brigade reserve and occasionally in divisional reserve in rest areas well behind the line.

Above: British trenches and wire by a trench known as Halifax Road, a long communication trench which ran from a point on the east bank of the Yser Canal opposite a position known as Marengo House near Bridge 6, up to the vicinity of Lancashire Farm. Lieutenant Hess would be wounded in the area near the centre of the photograph on 19th December 1915.

Chevaux de frises barbed wire obstacles stand sentinel in front of the parapets of the British trenches in the vicinity of Lancashire Farm. The rough grass and hedges of No Man's Land lie beyond, up to the breastworks of the German trenches on the Ypres – Pilckem road, clearly visible in front of the line of trees in the distance.

A real sense of desolation is captured perfectly in this study of No Man's Land.

SERGEANT YATES, D.C.M.

Sergeant John R. Yates, of 1, Station Road, Barnsley, who went into the firing line about four months ago, with the 1/5 Battalion York and Lancaster Regiment, has won the D.C.M. Sergeant Yates joined the army 22 years ago, and served 12 years with the colours before being invalided out of the army. He was in the Jameson Raid, and eight years was stationed in India. When discharged from the Army he returned to his home in Barnsley and worked as a colliery contractor at different district pits. In May last he enlisted in the Barnsley Territorials, and was the drummer in the band. He soon won his non-commissioned rank, and, according to letters sent home, his conduct at the front has been admirable. On one occasion he went out and gave aid to two wounded comrades, and succeeded in getting back safely to the British lines, despite the heavy fire of the enemy. His wife has received intimation of the honour he has won. At the present time Sergeant Yates is lying wounded in hospital in France, but his many Barnsley friends will be glad to hear he is making good progress.

This is a truly remarkable image taken looking northeast over the parapet of International Trench towards the extreme left of the British line. A communication trench can be seen to the left running past at least three white, wooden crosses marking front line graves and snaking towards the outposts of the British front line. Beyond the leafless trees in No Man's Land the German front line trench can be seen some 250 metres away in front of one of their strongpoints known as Farm 14 – 14 for no other reason than it stands 14 metres above sea level. Farm 14 was an 11 Brigade objective in its attack of 6th July but even after heavy fighting and the loss of International Trench which screened it, it remained in German hands.

Another view of Farm 14 behind the two trees in the centre of the photograph but this time Lieutenant Colver has moved a little way south along International Trench and the view is more to the north. The British forward trench is in the hollow and the Pilckem Ridge is in the distance.

By taking a photograph of the magnified image
reflected in a trench periscope, Lieutenant Colver
is able to record two 'close ups' of Farm 14.

Left: Second Lieutenant Morrell, the signalling officer in a trench on the Yser Canal. Morrell's nickname was 'Tiny' for obvious reasons.

Below: A Company men strike a serious pose. The man on the extreme left has been identified only by his nickname of 'Bushy' and the man on the extreme right smoking the pipe as Sergeant Roy Wardle. From 11th – 15th August 1915 German trench mortars were especially active on the extreme left of the line held by 1/5 near the Yser Canal where they did considerable damage to parapets. Casualties during this period were reported to be 'very heavy' amounting to twelve men killed and 35 wounded. Between 26th August and 19th September the battalion was alternately in support, again in the neighbourhood of Malakoff Farm, and the front line. During a spell in the fire trenches between 8th and 11th September the weather was very wet indeed and the trenches, especially the communication trenches, were in a very bad state as nothing had been done up to that point to drain them or to ensure that the surface water was carried away. Given the nature of the ground, the geology of the 'Wet Flanders Plain' beneath their feet and with autumn already upon them the men's chances of keeping their feet dry during tours of duty were decidedly slim.

On 18th September, A Company recovered two German trench mortars from International Trench which had been abandoned when the trench was captured by 11 Brigade. One of these was handed over to the trench howitzer school at Berthen and the other was sent back to England at Captain Colver's expense to be placed in the Drill Hall at Rotherham as a trophy. Here, machine gun officer Captain Rideal and an unidentified officer keep a low profile amidst the debris in International Trench next to the trench mortar which eventually found its way back to Britain. The weapon is a smoothbore 91mm *Lanz minenwerfer*, which was first manufactured in Mannheim early in 1915 by Heinrich Lanz. The Lanz, an 'auxiliary' trench weapon to the more usual range of trench mortars to be found in the German trenches, had a barrel of sheet steel and was mounted, as can be seen here, onto a reinforced wooden base which was then attached to a wooden sled. Depending on the type of projectile used, and it could fire several, it had a range of between 75 and 450 metres.

Right: Sergeant Olliphant is seen here examining the *Lanz minenwerfer*, during one of the battalion's periods in divisional reserve, prior to the weapon being sent back to Britain. He holds one of the *Lanz* projectiles in his left hand. Note the impact marks of at least a dozen rounds of small arms ammunition or shrapnel. It was far sighted of someone in the battalion or brigade to send the other German *minenwerfer* to the Second Army trench mortar school at Berthen. The school had been set up in order to teach infantry officers how to use the few British trench mortars which were slowly coming into service, when supplies of ammunition allowed, in response to the devastating effects that the German *minenwerfers* were having on the British trenches. A retired artillery captain, Sir J Keane, was the Commandant at Berthen assisted by Lieutenant Mitchell as Quartermaster/Adjutant along with two sergeant instructors.

Below: The *Lanz*, now back in Britain and with its sled removed, on display at the 1/5 York and Lancaster Regimental HQ at the Drill Hall in Rotherham, along with other trophies and weapons sent back by men of the 1/5 Battalion during their first year on the Western Front in Flanders in 1915.

It was during this period that the battalion lost nine men killed in action and Lieutenant Marcus Goodall and 50 men wounded. There was also another loss, as one of the battalion's most popular company commanders, Captain Hugh Parry-Smith, was invalided to England. On 26th September the 1/5 marched back to billets in farms and woods near Coppernolle Hoek, four kilometres north of Poperinghe and nine kilometres behind the front line, for a four-day spell in divisional reserve. These periods, relatively well away from danger, gave the men a chance to clean up, rest and recuperate after long periods of boredom punctuated by bouts of frenetic activity amid the constant dangers of snipers, shells or *minenwerfers* in the trenches. These bucolic scenes of peace and tranquillity are in stark contrast to the already barren conditions seen at the front line.

Two unidentified officers deep in conversation as they stroll in front of perfectly constructed 'show' trenches in the vicinity of Coppernolle Hoek.

Whilst in divisional reserve Lieutenant Colonel Fox's battalion HQ was established in a small hutment in the fields. Here Major Parkinson, (second on the right, hatless), chats with a small group of officers gathered at the doorway. An important announcement is due at any time and the senior officers are keen to have their photographs taken to mark the event.

Lieutenant Colonel Fox chose this period in divisional reserve to announce that he was relinquishing command of the battalion. He handed over temporary command to Major Knight on 28th September and left for home the same day. Fox had assumed command of the battalion on 1st April 1914 after Lieutenant Colonel Mitchell had stepped down. He had thus led his men, many of whom, particularly the officers, he regarded almost as family, into the greatest conflict the world had so far seen. Leaving the battalion must have caused mixed emotions.

He is pictured here with his trusted mainstays of his HQ, namely Major Knight (left) and his Adjutant, Major Parkinson.

Exemplifying the paternalistic nature of command of a Territorial Force battalion, Lieutenant Colonel Fox gathers his officers around him for a final group photograph before leaving for home. After six months on active service, there are several new faces amongst the ranks of the officers to replace the killed and wounded 'originals' of Fox's 'family' who entered the line near Fleurbaix in late April 1915. Harry Colver (middle row, seated extreme left) now sits to the right of Major Knight on the same row as the senior officers. As yet he wears no rank insignia on the sleeves of his tunic but he has been promoted Captain.

Inside Battalion HQ at Coppernolle Hoek, Lieutenant Colonel Fox (second from the right) is pictured here with Major Parkinson (in the far corner) and two of his remaining senior company officers, Captains Johnson (extreme left) and Colver (extreme right). Two unidentified officers, one of whom is with the Royal Engineers, join the group.

The HQ servants also have their photograph taken. The man on the right has been identified as Private Loder.

A replacement for Lieutenant Colonel Fox had at last been posted to the battalion and Lieutenant Colonel H A S Rendell took over command of the 1/5 York and Lancaster Regiment the following day. He did not have long to wait before taking his new command into the line.

Shortly after his arrival the new Commanding Officer of the 1/5 was photographed alongside the temporary CO, Major Knight.

A rifle with fixed bayonet is propped up in a trench near a dugout in the vicinity of Lancashire Farm during the autumn of 1915. As the autumn advanced so the conditions in the front line gradually worsened. In early October the battalion shuffled slightly south from their usual stretch of front line trenches and took over the left sector of the centre section of the line held by the 49th Division, with Battalion HQ at Lancashire Farm. Here the front line was further away from the canal bank as the Ypres Salient continued its bulge to the east. On 26th October there was some good news as Captain Stephen Rhodes rejoined the battalion after being out of action for several months. The next day the battalion went in for a four-day tour of duty and by now the conditions had become very poor. The front line itself was very wet with some of the trench walls falling in and some of the communication trenches almost impassable due to the high water levels. It rained almost continuously for the whole time and some of the fire bays were so flooded that they could only be held by a lone sentry. Not surprisingly the war diary remarked that the living conditions for all men were 'very bad' and most of the time was spent in clearing away falls of earth and patching up.

(Courtesy York and Lancaster Regimental Museum)

More rifles propped up against the forward wall of a fire trench. It would appear that this image was taken during a relatively fine period, as the floor of the trench looks dry. (Courtesy York and Lancaster Regimental Museum)

Captain Harry Colver peeps out of his dugout in a very cramped section of the line. (Courtesy York and Lancaster Regimental Museum)

Packed in like sardines these young men of A Company in the foreground do not have much room for manoeuvre. Further along the trench another man is able to sit on the firestep and place his feet onto the opposite wall to stretch out. (Courtesy York and Lancaster Regimental Museum)

Experienced men. Further along the trench Captain Colver snaps a pair of seasoned NCOs. The man on the left has a pair of goggles pushed up over his hat-band to be pulled down over the eyes in case of an attack with tear producing lachrymatory shells.

Two A Company men (left) manage to raise a smile for Captain Colver during a smoke break. Lieutenant Colver has no such luck with these men (below) who have resignation written all over their faces. Boredom was just one more enemy to contend with in the trenches of Flanders in 1915.
(Courtesy York and Lancaster Regimental Museum)

More men of the 1/5 combat the boredom in the trenches while one man tries to catch up on some sleep. On 3rd November it was the turn of another of the battalion's original officers to depart when Major Parkinson received orders to proceed to England. Captain Rhodes duly took over the duties of Adjutant on November 4th.

In another image (opposite) in which the men of A Company more closely resemble brigands and pirates than British soldiers – note the man in the centre of the group of three with the scarf wrapped around his head – these men from Rotherham succeed in striking a warlike pose for Captain Colver whilst they hold what could be argued to be the worst stretch of line in the Ypres Salient. Two of the men hold rifle grenades whilst another takes a nap on the floor of the trench covered with a greatcoat. As November gave way to December, while the numbers of killed and wounded continued to rise inexorably, the conditions in the trenches deteriorated still further. In some places the water was three feet deep. The history of the 1/4 Battalion of the York and Lancaster Regiment records that the '...continuous exposure to heavy fire in the most unpleasant mud and water reduced the stay at Ypres to a dead level of monotony.'[10] But the monotony was soon to be relieved as the Germans prepared to register another first in the history of warfare. A German NCO was captured on the night of the 4th /5th December who offered the information that gas cylinders had been dug into the front of the XXVI Reserve Corps for some time while intelligence picked up another source that warned of a gas attack somewhere in Flanders sometime after 10th December when the conditions were favourable. Facing the German XXVI Corps on the other side of No Man's Land for the greater part of its front was the 6th Division and – under the command of Major General E M Perceval after the wounding of Major General Baldock – the 49th (West Riding) Division.[11]

At 5.00 am On 19th December, 1915 a single light was seen to shoot up from the German lines in the darkness and descend slowly on a parachute. Fifteen minutes later red rockets splintered the night sky all along the German front arousing much suspicion amongst British sentries, many of whom woke their officers. On the front of the 49th Division a bout of heavy rifle fire from the German lines was followed, at about 5.25 am, by a strange hissing noise, accompanied almost immediately by an odour reminiscent of mouldy hay. On 22nd April 1915 the Germans had used chlorine cloud gas as a weapon for the first time in history, now they were intent on another first but this time using a mix of chlorine and phosgene, the first time phosgene had been used as a weapon of war. With the British already on 'gas alert', klaxons, bells, gongs and shell cases were sounded and the 1/5 York and Lancs, alongside 1/4 KOYLI in the centre of the 49th divisional front, donned their recently issued P helmets, manned their parapets and opened fire on the German lines to deter any possible attack. On the front of the 1/5, heavy shelling started at 5.45 am, continued until 9.00 am and after that went on intermittently all day. But mixed in with the high explosive were phosgene gas shells, which, because they heralded their arrival with merely a 'dull splash', took many officers and men unawares. Although the original gas cloud – fifteen metres high and moving quickly on a freshening north east wind – fanned out over a broad area to the south east of Ypres and passed away in half an hour, the arrival of gas shells added to the concentrations already in the atmosphere. The P helmets were not able to cope with phosgene in high concentrations and by the time some garrisons knew what was happening as the gas shells began plopping down around them, the damage had already been done. The effect of phosgene is similar to chlorine but is far more dangerous since it causes less irritation to the senses and so can be inhaled for quite a long time at quite high concentrations without any severe signs of distress or discomfort. There may be nausea, coughing or vomiting but these symptoms eventually pass only for the sufferer to become seriously ill a day or so later and in the worst cases, die as they drown in the fluid produced in their lungs due to the effects of the gas.[12]

By 6.30 am on the morning of 19th December, the order, 'attack move' was sent out to the support companies of the 1/5 and half of each was sent forward. At the same time 148 Brigade reserves began to move but were halted as a full scale German attack failed to materialise. Pre-arranged defensive schemes were also set in train in other brigades of the 49th Division and throughout the 6th Division while the 14th Division in VI Corps reserve was ordered to stand-to. Opposite the 1/5 no attack developed. A few men were seen to leave the German lines – patrols sent out to try and ascertain the effects of the gas – but these were 'sniped' and went to ground. By around 9.30 am, an hour and a half after daybreak, British units were reporting that the situation was under control and almost back to normal. The British line had held firm. The damage to the 1/5 front and support trenches was reported as 'slight' but the casualties were heavy indeed. Twenty-three year old Captain Colver and Second Lieutenants D Childe and H Hardaker had been killed by gas with another four suffering from its effects and one wounded. Six other ranks had died from the effects of gas, with two killed by bullets and three from shellfire, 23 men had been wounded and 87 were suffering from gas inhalation. One man had been wounded and was also suffering from the effects of the gas: a battalion total of 130. Total British casualties from gas amounted to 1,069 of which 120 were fatalities, with three-quarters of them in the 49th Division.[13] And with the death of Captain Colver, so ended a remarkable photographic record of a Territorial battalion marching off to war and serving in the trenches of Flanders during 1915. If his brother officers took any further images they have not so far come to light.

On the night of 19th December the 1/5 was relieved by 1/7 Battalion West Riding Regiment and marched back to a rest camp near Coppernolle Woods. A large number of men were suffering severely from bronchial trouble and only one officer per company was fit for duty. Even so the battalion was ordered back into the support line again on 20th December but could only muster 290 of all ranks of which 100 still felt unwell! Two days before Christmas the battalion went back into the front line trenches of this sector of the Ypres Salient for the last time and held the entire line in small groups of just six men. Their gloom was partially relieved with the presence of officers of the 24th Division who were touring the trenches with a view to taking them over. Hopes were raised. Would the battalion soon be on the move? The war diary records that there was some attempt at 'fraternisation' by the Germans on Christmas Eve but in the light of recent events it was 'suppressed firmly' in a hail of bullets. Christmas Day 1915 was spent in the trenches and was described as a quiet day although Second Lieutenant Elliott was wounded. The battalion heard that the 14th (Light) Divison would in fact be relieving the 49th and on 27th December the battalion drove away from the Salient in motor buses, arriving first at Steenvoorde at 5.00 am on 29th December before finally arriving at a camp on the Dunkirk road east of Calais, where they rested as 1915 passed into 1916. So ended, according to Major General Perceval, in a letter circulated to his 49th Division, almost six months duty, *'in the worst trenches of the Allied lines during the whole of which period, the men had unflinchingly sustained an unrelaxed bombardment and had borne with unfailing cheerfulness the most trying conditions of weather in permanently flooded trenches.'*[14]

There was more, much more fighting ahead for the 1/5 York and Lancaster Regiment and the 49th Division in the years to come but its service in Flanders in 1915 had, like Captain Harry Colver's photographic odyssey, finally come to an end.

The original grave of Captain Harry Colver in Bard Cottage cemetery: a photograph taken after the war by a member of his family. The cemetery – the chosen site was in a sheltered position beneath a high bank – was begun in June 1915 and was named after a house on the west bank of the Yperlee River close to a bridge called Bard's Causeway. Burials were made in the cemetery up until October 1918. Captain Colver's grave can still be found in Bard Cottage cemetery, a good deal larger now than during the war years, in the first row of the first plot, although it is now cared for by the Commonwealth War Graves Commission.

Notes on Sources

Introduction
1 Keegan J and Knightley, P, *The Eye of War: Words and Photographs from the Front Line*, pp 6-7
2 Ibid, pp 7-8

Part 1 – Mobilisation
1 Messenger, *A Call to Arms – The British Army 1914-18*, pp 70-75
2 Magnus, *The West Riding Territorials in the Great War*, pp 30, 39-40
3 1/5 York and Lancaster Regiment War Diary, National Archives, WO 95/2805
4 Messenger, op.cit., pp 82-3
5 Ibid, p 81, see also Grant, Captain D P *The 1/4 (Hallamshire) Battalion, York and Lancaster Regiment, 1914 -1919* (privately published) p13

Part 2 – War in French Flanders – Fleurbaix
1 Grant, p15
2 Correspondence Sir Henry Rawlinson to Lord Kitchener, Secretary of State for War. The National Archives, PRO 30 57/51
3 *The Barnsley Chronicle*, May 29th 1915
4 Barton, Peter, Doyle, Peter and Vandewalle, Johan, *Beneath Flanders Fields: The Tunnellers' War 1914-18* (Staplehurst: Spellmount, 2005) pp 14-15
5 1/5 York and Lancaster Regiment War Diary, National Archives, WO 95/2805
6 Edmonds, Brigadier-General J E and Wynne, Captain G C, *Military Operations France and Belgium 1915*, Vol. 1, (London: MacMillan, 1927) pp vi- vii
7 Grant, op.cit., pp 15-16
8 Keegan, *The First World War*, pp 213-215, Simkins, Peter, *World War 1 1914-18: The Western Front* p 63
9 Grant, op.cit., p16
10 1/5 York and Lancaster Regiment War Diary, National Archives, WO 95/2805
11 Magnus, op.cit., p 53

Part 3 – 'The Worst Trenches of the Allied Line.' The Ypres Salient
1 1/5 York and Lancaster Regiment War Diary, National Archives, WO 95/2805
2 Grant, op.cit., p 23
3 Hughes, Simon, Operations on the Yser Canal: The 1st Battalion Somerset Light Infantry and an analysis of its part in the attack on International Trench, 6th July 1915, The Western Front Association, Contributed Articles, www.westernfront.co.uk/thegreatwar/articles/research/yser1
4 Cave, *Battleground Europe*, p 148
5 Ibid, p 150
6 Ibid, p 151
7 1/5 York and Lancaster Regiment War Diary, National Archives, WO 95/2805
8 Hughes, op.cit.
9 Cooksey, Jon, *Pals: The 13th and 14th Battalions of the York and Lancaster Regiment*, p 94
10 Grant, op.cit., p 24
11 Edmonds, *Military Operations France and Belgium 1916*, Vol. 1, p 158
12 Ibid, p 79
13 Ibid, p 161
14 Magnus, op.cit., p 64

Bibliography

Barton, Peter, Doyle, Peter and Vandewalle, Johan, *Beneath Flanders Fields: The Tunnellers' War 1914-18*, (Staplehurst: Spellmount, 2005)
Cave, Nigel, *Battleground Europe*, (Barnsley: Wharncliffe Publishing, 1990)
Cooksey, Jon, *Pals: The 13th and 14th Battalions of the York and Lancaster Regiment*, (Barnsley: Pen and Sword, 1996)
Edmonds, Brigadier-General J E and Wynne, Captain G C, *Military Operations France and Belgium 1915*, Vol. 1, (London: MacMillan, 1927)
Edmonds, Brigadier-General J E, *Military Operations France and Belgium 1916*, Vol. 1, (London: MacMillan, 1932)
Grant, Captain D P, *The 1/4 (Hallamshire) Battalion, York and Lancaster Regiment, 1914 -1919*, (privately published)
Keegan, John, *The First World War*, (London: Hutchinson, 1998)
Keegan, John and Knightley, Phillip, *The Eye of War: Words and Photographs from the Front Line*, (London: Weidenfeld and Nicolson, 2003)
Magnus, Laurie, *The West Riding Territorials in the Great War*, (London: Kegan Paul, Trench, Trubner, 1920)
Messenger, Charles, *A Call to Arms: The British Army 1914-18*, (London: Weidenfeld and Nicolson, 2005)
Simkins, Peter, *World War 1 1914-18: The Western Front*, (Godalming: CLB, 1992)